"And they overcame him by the blood of the Lamb, and by the word of their testimony; and they loved not their lives unto death."

Revelation 12:11

Foxe's Christian Martyrs of the World

John Foxe

A Barbour Book

ISBN 1-55748-456-2

FOXE'S CHRISTIAN MARTYRS OF THE WORLD

PRINTED IN THE U.S.A.

Introduction

John Foxe was born in 1516, in Boston, Lincolnshire, England. At the age of sixteen, he went to Oxford, where he received his B.A. in 1537, became a professor, and completed his masters in 1543. While teaching at Oxford, he became good friends with Hugh Latimer and William Tyndale, embracing Protestantism. His views were more extreme than his college allowed, so he left the university in 1545, married, and moved to London, where he became the tutor of the duke of Norfolk's grandchildren.

Foxe was ordained a deacon of the Church of England and worked for the Reformation, writing several tracts and beginning work on his account of Christian martyrs, but was forced to leave the country in 1553 when the Catholic Queen Mary took the throne. The first part of his book was published in 1554, in Strassburg, France. He then went to Frankfurt to support John Knox's Calvinistic party and moved to Basel, Switzerland, where he served as a printer's proofreader.

Manuscripts and eye-witness accounts of the Protestants' persecution under Queen Mary were forwarded to Foxe in Basel, and he continued to work on his book, publishing the completed manuscript in 1559, the year after Queen Elizabeth I took the throne. Returning to England, he filled in more details, translated the book into English, and printed it in March of 1563 under the title _Actes and monuments of these latter and perillous days._

Becoming popularly known as _The Book of Martyrs,_ the text was widely ready by English Puritans, shaping popular opinion about Catholicism for at least a century.

Foxe was ordained an Anglican priest in 1560 but refused all church offices because of his Puritan beliefs. He continued to preach and publish his sermons, however, ministered to the victims of the plague of 1563, then begged Queen Elizabeth not to execute the Anabaptists in 1575 and the Jesuits in 1581.

Meanwhile, _The Book of Martyrs_ was installed in English churches, read to the shipmates of Sir Francis Drake, and studied by Puritan families, who considered it a vital part of the education of their children.

Foxe died in April 1587 and was buried at St. Gile's Church, Cripplegate, London. His wife survived him by eighteen years; they had at least five children.

This edition is a retelling of Foxe's major stories in modern English, and should be readily understandable by both children and adults.

1

Persecution of the Early Christians

In the gospel of Matthew we read that Simon Peter was the first person to openly acknowledge Jesus as the Son of God and that Jesus, seeing God's hand in this acknowledgment, called Peter a rock on which He would build His Church — a Church that even the gates of hell would not be able to defeat.

This indicates three things. First, that Christ will have a Church in this world. Secondly, that the Church would be persecuted, not only by the world, but also by all the powers of hell. Thirdly, despite its persecutions, the Church would survive.

The whole history of the Church to this day verifies this prophecy of Christ. Princes, kings, and other rulers of this world have used all their strength and cunning against the Church, yet it continues to endure and hold its own. The storms it has overcome are remarkable. I have written this history so the wonderful works of God within the Church will be visible to all who might profit from them.

Of all the people who heard Jesus speak, the Pharisees and scribes should have been the first to accept Him, since they were so familiar with God's law. Yet they persecuted and rejected Him, choosing to remain subject to Caesar, and it was Caesar who eventually destroyed them.

God's punishment also fell heavily on the Romans. Hearing of Christ's works, death, and resurrection, emperor Tiberius proposed to the Roman senate that He be adored as God, but the senators refused, preferring the emperor to the King of heaven. In reply, God stirred their own emperors against them, causing most of the senate to be destroyed and the city of Rome to be afflicted for nearly three hundred years.

Tiberius became a tyrant, killing his own mother, his nephews, the princes of the city, and his own counselors. Seutonius reported him to be so stern that one day alone he saw twenty people executed. Pilate, under whom Christ was crucified, was sent to Rome and banished to the town of Vienne, in Dauphiny, where he eventually committed suicide. Agrippa the elder was even imprisoned by Tiberius for some time.

After Tiberius's death came Caligula, who demanded to be worshiped as a god. He banished Herod Antipas, the murderer of John the Baptist and condemner of Christ, and was assassinated in the fourth year of his reign.

Following thirteen cruel years under Claudius, the people of Rome fell under the power of Nero, who reigned for fourteen years, killing most of the Roman senate and destroying the whole Roman order of knighthood. He was so cruel and inhumane that he put to death his own mother, his brother-in-law, his sister, his wife, and his instructors, Seneca and Lucan. Then he ordered Rome set on fire in twelve places while he sang the verses of Homer. To avoid the blame for this, he accused the Christians of setting the fires and caused them to be persecuted.

In the year A.D. 70, Titus and his father Vespasian destroyed Jerusalem and all of Galilee, killing over 1,100,000 Jews and selling the rest into slavery. So we see that those who refused Jesus were made to suffer for their actions.

The Apostles

The first apostle to suffer after the martyrdom of Stephen was James, the brother of John. Clement tells us, "When this James was brought to the tribunal seat, he that brought him and was the cause of his trouble, seeing him to be condemned and that he should suffer death, was in such sort moved within heart and conscience that as he went to the execution he confessed himself also, of his own accord, to be a Christian. And so were they led forth together, where in the way he desired of James to forgive him what he had done. After James had a little paused with himself upon the matter, turning to him he said, 'Peace be to thee, brother;' and kissed him. And both were beheaded together, A.D. 36."

Thomas preached to the Parthians, Medes, Persians, Carmanians, Hyrcanians, Bactrians, and Magians. He was killed in Calamina, India.

Simon, brother of Jude and James the younger, who were all the sons of Mary Cleophas and Alpheus, was Bishop of Jerusalem after James. He was crucified in Egypt during the reign of the Roman emperor Trajan.

Simon the apostle, called Cananeus and Zelotes, preached in Mauritania, Africa, and Britain. He was also crucified.

Mark, the first Bishop of Alexandria, preached the gospel in Egypt. He was burned and buried in a place named Bucolus during Trajan's reign.

Bartholomew is said to have preached in India and translated the gospel of Matthew into their tongue. He was beaten, crucified, and beheaded in Albinopolis, Armenia.

Andrew, Peter's brother, preached to the Scythians, Sogdians, and the Sacae in Sebastopolis, Ethiopia, in the year A.D. 80. He was crucified by Aegeas, the governor of the Edessenes, and buried in Patrae, in Archaia. Bernard and St. Cyprian mention the confession and martyrdom of this blessed apostle. Partly from them and partly from other reliable writers, we gather the following material.

When Andrew, through his diligent preaching, had brought many to the faith of Christ, Aegeas the governor asked permission of the Roman senate to force all Christians to sacrifice to and honor the Roman idols. Andrew thought he should resist Aegeas and went to him, telling him that a judge of men should first know and worship his Judge in heaven. While worshiping the true God, Andrew said, he should banish all false gods and blind idols from his mind.

Furious at Andrew, Aegeas demanded to know if he was the man who had recently overthrown the temple of the gods and persuaded men to become Christians — a "superstitious sect" that had recently been declared illegal by the Romans.

Andrew replied that the rulers of Rome didn't understand the truth. The Son of God, who came into the world for man's sake, taught that the Roman gods were devils, enemies of mankind, teaching men to offend God and causing Him to turn away from them. By serving the devil, men fall into all kinds of wickedness, Andrew said, and after they die, nothing but their evil deeds are remembered.

The proconsul ordered Andrew not to preach these things any more or he would face a speedy crucifixion. Whereupon Andrew replied, "I would not have preached the honor and glory of the cross if I feared the death of the cross." He was condemned to be crucified for teaching a new sect and taking away the religion of the Roman gods.

Andrew, going toward the place of execution and seeing the cross waiting for him, never changed his expression. Neither did he fail in his speech. His body fainted not, nor did his reason fail him, as often happens to men about to die. He said, "O cross, most welcome and longed for! With a willing mind, joyfully and desirously, I come to you, being the scholar of Him which did hang on you, because I have always been your lover and yearned to embrace you."

Matthew wrote his gospel to the Jews in the Hebrew tongue. After he had converted Ethiopia and all Egypt, Hircanus the king sent someone to kill him with a spear.

After years of preaching to the barbarous nations, Philip was stoned and crucified in Hierapolis, Phrygia, and buried there with his daughter.

Of James, the brother of the Lord, we read the following. James, being considered a just and perfect man, governed the Church with the apostles. He drank no wine or any strong drink, ate no meat, and never shaved his head. He was the only man allowed to enter into the holy place, for he never wore wool, just linen. He would enter into the temple alone, fall on his knees, and ask remission for the people, doing this so often that his knees lost their sense of feeling and became hardened, like the knees of a camel. Because of his holy life, James was called "The Just" and "the safeguard of the people."

When many of their chief men had been converted, the Jews, scribes, and Pharisees began to fear that soon all the people would decide to follow Jesus. They met with James, saying, "We beg you to restrain the people, for they believe Jesus as though he were Christ. Persuade those who come to

the passover to think correctly about Christ, because they will
all listen to you. Stand on the top of the temple so you can be
heard by everyone."

During passover the scribes and Pharisees put James on
top of the temple, calling out to him, "You just man, whom we
all ought to obey, this people is going astray after Jesus, who
was crucified."

And James answered, "Why do you ask me of Jesus the
Son of Man? He sits on the right hand of the Most High, and
shall come in the clouds of heaven."

Hearing this, many in the crowd were persuaded and
glorified God, crying, "Hosannah to the Son of David!"

Then the scribes and Pharisees realized they had done the
wrong thing by allowing James to testify of Christ. They cried
out, "Oh, this just man is seduced, too!" then went up and
threw James off the temple.

But James wasn't killed by the fall. He turned, fell on his
knees, and called, "O Lord God, Father, I beg You to forgive
them, for they know not what they do."

They decided to stone James, but a priest said to them,
"Wait! What are you doing? The just man is praying for you!"
But one of the men there — a fuller — took the instrument
he used to beat cloth and hit James on the head, killing him,
and they buried him where he fell. James was a true witness
for Christ to the Jews and the Gentiles.

The First Persecution

The first of the ten persecutions was stirred up by Nero
about A.D. 64. His rage against the Christians was so fierce that
Eusebius records, "a man might then see cities full of men's
bodies, the old lying together with the young, and the dead

bodies of women cast out naked, without reverence of that sex, in the open streets." Many Christians in those days thought that Nero was the antichrist because of his cruelty and abominations.

The apostle Peter was condemned to death during this persecution, although some say he escaped. It is known that many Christians encouraged him to leave the city, and the story goes that as he came to the city's gate, Peter saw Jesus coming to meet him. "Lord, where are You going?" Peter asked.

"I am come again to be crucified," was the answer.

Seeing that his suffering was understood, Peter returned to the city, where Jerome tells us he was crucified head down at his own request, saying he was not worthy to be crucified the same way his Lord was.

Paul also suffered under this persecution when Nero sent two of his esquires, Ferega and Parthemius, to bring him to his execution. They found Paul instructing the people and asked him to pray for them, so they might believe. Receiving Paul's assurance that they would soon be baptized, the two men led him out of the city to the place of execution, where Paul was beheaded. This persecution ended under Vespasian's reign, giving the Christians a little peace.

The Second Persecution

The second persecution began during the reign of Domitian, the brother of Titus. Domitian exiled John to the island of Patmos, but on Domitian's death John was allowed to return to Ephesus in the year A.D. 97. He remained there until the reign of Trajan, governing the churches in Asia and writing his gospel until he died at about the age of one hundred.

. Why did the Roman emperors and senate persecute the Christians so? First of all, they didn't understand that Christ's kingdom is not a temporal kingdom and they feared for their powerful leadership roles if too many citizens followed Christ. Secondly, Christians despised the false Roman gods, preferring to worship only the true, living God. Whatever happened in Rome — famine, disease, earthquake, wars, bad weather — was blamed on the Christians who defied the Roman gods.

Death was not considered enough punishment for the Christians, who were subjected to the cruelest treatment possible. They were whipped, disemboweled, torn apart, and stoned. Plates of hot iron were laid on them; they were strangled, eaten by wild animals, hung, and tossed on the horns of bulls. After they were dead, their bodies were piled in heaps and left to rot without burial. Nevertheless, the Church continued to grow, deeply rooted in the doctrine of the apostles and watered with the blood of the saints.

The Third Persecution

During the third persecution, Pliny the second wrote to the emperor Trajan, complaining that thousands of Christians were being killed daily, although none of them had done anything worthy of persecution.

During this persecution Ignatius was condemned to death because he professed Christ. At the time, he was living in Antioch, next in line as bishop after Peter. As he made the trip from Syria to Rome under heavy guard, he preached to the churches he passed and asked the church in Rome not to try to save him. Condemned to be thrown to the lions, Ignatius replied, "I am the wheat of Christ: I am going to be ground with the teeth of wild beasts, that I may be found pure bread."

The Fourth Persecution

After a respite, the Christians again came under persecution, this time from Marcus Aurelius, in A.D. 161.

One of those who suffered this time was Polycarp, the venerable bishop of Smyrna. Three days before he was captured, Polycarp dreamed that a pillow under his head caught fire, and when he awoke, he told those around him that he would burn alive for Christ's sake.

Hearing his captors had arrived one evening, Polycarp left his bed to welcome them, ordered a meal prepared for them, and then asked for an hour alone to pray. The soldiers were so impressed by Polycarp's advanced age and composure that they began to wonder why they had been sent to take him, but as soon as he had finished his prayers, they put him on an ass and brought him to the city.

As he entered the stadium with his guards, a voice from heaven was heard to say, "Be strong, Polycarp, and play the man." No one nearby saw anyone speaking, but many people heard the voice.

Brought before the tribunal and the crowd, Polycarp refused to deny Christ, although the proconsul begged him to "consider yourself and have pity on your great age. Reproach Christ and I will release you."

Polycarp replied, "Eighty-six years I have served Him, and He never once wronged me. How can I blaspheme my King, who saved me?"

Threatened with wild beasts and fire, Polycarp stood his ground. "What are you waiting for? Do whatever you please."

The crowd demanded Polycarp's death, gathering wood for the fire and preparing to tie him to the stake.

"Leave me," he said. "He who will give me strength to sustain the fire will help me not to flinch from the pile." So they bound him but didn't nail him to the stake. As soon as Polycarp finished his prayer, the fire was lit, but it leaped up around him, leaving him unburned, until the people convinced a soldier to plunge a sword into him. When he did, so much blood gushed out that the fire was immediately extinguished. The soldiers then placed his body into a fire and burned it to ashes, which some Christians later gathered up and buried properly.

In this same persecution, the Christians of Lyons and Vienne, two cities in France, also suffered, including Sanctus of Vienne, Maturus, Attalus of Pergamos, and the woman Blandina, all of whom endured extreme torture and death with fortitude and grace.

The Fifth Persecution, A.D. 200

During the reign of Severus, the Christians had several years of rest and could worship God without fear of punishment. But after a time, the hatred of the ignorant mob again prevailed, and the old laws were remembered and put in force against them. Fire, sword, wild beasts, and imprisonment were resorted to again, and even the dead bodies of Christians were stolen from their graves and mutilated. Yet the faithful continued to multiply. Tertullian, who lived at this time, said that if the Christians had all gone away from the Roman territories, the empire would have been greatly weakened.

By now, the persecutions had extended to northern Africa, which was a Roman province, and many were murdered in that area. One of these was Perpetua, a married lady twenty-six years old with a baby at her breast. On being taken before the proconsul Minutius, Perpetua was commanded to sacrifice to the idols. Refusing to do so, she was put in a dark dungeon and deprived of her child, but two of her keepers, Tertius and Pomponius, allowed her out in the fresh air several hours a day, during which time she was allowed to nurse her child.

Finally the Christians were summoned to appear before the judge and urged to deny their Lord, but all remained firm. When Perpetua's turn came, her father suddenly appeared, carrying her infant in his arms, and begged her to save her own life for the sake of her child. Even the judge seemed to be moved. "Spare the gray hairs of your father," he said. "Spare your child. Offer sacrifice for the welfare of the emperor."

Perpetua answered, "I will not sacrifice."

"Are you a Christian?" demanded Hilarianus, the judge.

"I am a Christian," was her answer.

Perpetua and all the other Christians tried with her that day were ordered killed by wild beasts as a show for the crowd on the next holiday. They entered the place of execution clad in the simplest of robes, Perpetua singing a hymn of triumph. The men were to be torn to pieces by leopards and bears. Perpetua and a young woman named Felicitas were hung up in nets, at first naked, but the crowd demanded that they should be allowed their clothing.

When they were again returned to the arena, a bull was let loose on them. Felicitas fell, seriously wounded. Perpetua was tossed, her loose robe torn and her hair falling loose, but she hastened to the side of the dying Felicitas and gently raised her from the ground. When the bull refused to attack them again, they were dragged out of the arena, to the disappointment of the crowd, which wanted to see their deaths. Finally brought back in to be killed by gladiators, Perpetua was assigned to a trembling young man who stabbed her weakly several times, not being used to such scenes of violence. When she saw how upset the young man was, Perpetua guided his sword to a vital area and died.

The Sixth Persecution, A.D. 235

This persecution was begun by the emperor Maximinus, who ordered all Christians hunted down and killed. A Roman soldier who refused to wear a laurel crown bestowed on him by the emperor and confessed he was a Christian was scourged, imprisoned, and put to death.

Pontianus, Bishop of Rome, was banished to Sardinia for preaching against idolatry and murdered. Anteros, a Grecian who succeeded Pontianus as Bishop of Rome, collected a history of the martyrs and suffered martyrdom himself after only forty days in office.

Pammachius, a Roman senator, and forty-two other Christians were all beheaded in one day and their heads set on the city gates. Calepodius, a Christian minister, after being dragged through the streets, was thrown into the Tiber River with a millstone fastened around his neck. Quiritus, a Roman nobleman, and his family and servants, was barbarously tortured and put to death. Martina, a noble young lady, was beheaded, and Hippolitus, a Christian prelate, was tied to a wild horse and dragged through fields until he died.

Maximinus was succeeded by Gordian, during whose reign and that of his successor, Philip, the Church was free from persecution for more than six years. But in 249, a violent persecution broke out in Alexandria without the emperor's knowledge.

Metrus, an old Christian of Alexandria, refused to worship idols. He was beaten with clubs, pricked with sharp reeds, at stoned to death. Quinta, a Christian woman was dragged by her feet over sharp flint stones, scourged with whips, and finally stoned to death. Apollonia, an old woman nearly seventy, confessed that she was a Christian, and the mob fastened her to a stake, preparing to burn her. She begged to be let loose and the mob untied her, thinking she was ready to recant, but to their astonishment, she immediately threw herself back into the flames and died.

The Seventh Persecution, A.D. 249

By now, the heathen temples of Rome were almost forsaken, and the Christian churches were crowded with converts. The emperor Decius decided it was time to crush the Christians once and for all.

Fabian, the Bishop of Rome, was the first person of authority to feel the severity of this persecution. The former emperor, Philip, had put his treasure into the care of Fabian. When Decius examined the treasure, there was far less than he had expected, so he had Fabian arrested and beheaded.

Decius, having built a pagan temple at Ephesus, commanded everyone in the city to sacrifice to its idols. This order was refused by seven of his own soldiers: Maximianus, Martianus, Joannes, Malchus, Dionysius, Constantinus, and Seraion. The emperor, willing to try a little persuasion, gave them tine to consider until her returned from a journey, but in his absence they escaped and hid in a cave. Decius was told of this on his return, and the mouth of the cave was closed up, so all seven soldiers starved to death.

Theodora, a beautiful young lady of Antioch, refused to sacrifice to the Roman idols and was condemned to prison. Didymus, her Christian lover, disguised himself as a Roman soldier and went to Theodora's cell, where he convinced her to put on his armor and escape. When he was discovered, Didymus was taken to the governor and condemned to death. When she heard Didymus's sentence, Theodora threw herself at the judge's feet and begged that she be the one to suffer, not Didymus. The judge ordered them both beheaded and their bodies burned.

Origen, the celebrated author and teacher of Alexandria was arrested at the age of sixty-four and thrown into prison in chains, his feet placed in the stocks, which held his legs stretched widely apart. Even though Origen was rich and famous, he received no mercy. He was threatened by fire and tormented by every means available, but his fortitude carried him through it all, even when his judge ordered the torturers to prolong his suffering. During the torture, Decius died and his successor began a war with the Goths, which turned the empire's attention away from the Christians. Origen was freed; he lived in Tyre until he died at the age of sixty-nine.

2

The Eighth Persecution, A.D. 257

When Valerian was first made emperor, he was moderate and kind to the Christians, but then he fell under the influence of an Egyptian magician named Macrianus and ordered the persecutions to continue, which they did for the next three years and six months.

Stephen, the Bishop of Rome, was beheaded, and Saturnius, Bishop of Toulouse, was attacked and seized by the crowd there for preventing the oracles from speaking. On refusing to sacrifice to the idols, he was fastened by the feet to the tail of a bull, which was then driven down the steps of the temple, dragging Saturnius until his head opened and his brains fell out. None of the Christians in Toulouse had the courage to carry away his dead body until two women took it and buried it in a ditch.

In Rome, Lawrence was brought before the authorities, who knew he was not only a minister of the sacraments but also a distributor of the Church's riches. When they demanded he hand over all the Church possessed, Lawrence asked for three days to collect it. On the third day, when the persecutor demanded the wealth of the Church, Lawrence stretched his arms out over a group of poor Christians he'd gathered together. "These are the precious treasure of the Church," he told his judge. "What more precious jewels can Christ have than those in whom He promised to dwell?"

Furious at being tricked and out of his mind with anger, Lawrence's persecutor ordered him whipped, beaten, tied to burning-hot plates of iron, then laid on a bed of iron over a fire and roasted alive.

The first English martyr was a man named Alban, who was converted by a poor clerk who took shelter in his house. When the authorities eventually came for the clerk, Alban dressed in his clothes and went in his place. The judge recognized Alban and demanded he sacrifice to his heathen gods or die. When Alban refused, he was tortured and beheaded.

The Ninth Persecution, A.D. 270

This persecution began under the emperor Aurelian. Among those who suffered at this time was Felix, Bishop of Rome, who was beheaded. Agapetus, a young Roman who sold his estate and gave the money to the poor, was seized as a Christian, tortured, and then brought to Praeneste, a city near Rome, where he was beheaded. These are the only martyrs whose names were recorded during this reign.

The Tenth Persecution, A.D. 303

In the beginning of the tenth persecution, which was in the nineteenth year of his reign, the emperor Dioclesian appointed Maximian to share his throne with him, and the two of them chose Galerius and Constantius to serve under them. Under these rulers the Christians were again persecuted furiously, a state that would continue until A.D. 313, even though Dioclesian and Maximian gave up their offices in the year A.D. 305.

Constantius and Galerius divided the empire between them, Galerius taking the eastern countries and Constantius ruling France, Spain, and Britain. Meanwhile, the Roman soldiers set up Maxentius as their Caesar in Rome. While Galerius and Maxentius continued the persecution for seven or eight years, Constantius became a supporter of the Christians in his empire, being an enlightened, intelligent ruler who was always concerned for the welfare of his subjects, never waging unjust wars or aiding those who did. Churches were terribly persecuted in other parts of the empire, but Constantius gave Christians the freedom to live and worship as they chose, even appointing them as his closest protectors and advisors.

Constantius died in A.D. 306 and was buried at York, England. His son Constantine, an English-born Christian, succeeded him — a ruler every bit as compassionate and dedicated as his father.

In Rome, Maxentius was ruling as a tyrant, killing his own noblemen, confiscating their goods for himself, and practicing magic — the only thing he seemed to do well. In the beginning of his reign he pretended to be a friend of the Christians, but only to win popular support while he secretly continued the persecution.

The citizens and senators of Rome soon grew weary of Maxentius's tyranny and wickedness and petitioned Constantine to come free them. At first Constantine tried to convince Maxentius to mend his ways, but when that had no effect, he gathered an army in Britain and France and began marching toward Italy in A.D. 313.

Knowing he didn't have the support of his people, Maxentius had to rely on his magic arts and occasional ambushes of Constantine's advancing army, neither of which slowed Constantine's advance toward Rome.

But as he neared Rome, Constantine began to feel nervous about the coming battle. He'd seen Maxentius defeat others by the use of his magic, and he wished he had a force he could use against it. One day at sunset, Constantine looked up to the south to see the bright form of the cross and the words, "In this overcome." He and the men with him were astonished at the sign, although no one was too sure what it actually meant. But one night as Constantine slept, Christ appeared to him with the same cross, telling him to make a cross to carry before him into battle.

This sign and its message wasn't given to induce superstitious worship of the cross, as though the cross had any power in itself, but as an admonition to seek Jesus and set forth the glory of His name.

The next day Constantine had a cross made of gold and precious stones, which he had carried before the army in place of his flag. With added confidence that God had blessed his cause, he hurried toward Rome and the showdown with Maxentius.

Maxentius was now forced out of the city to meet Constantine on the far side of the Tiber River. After he crossed the bridge named Pons Milvius, Maxentius destroyed it, replacing it with an unstable bridge made of boats and planks, thinking to trap Constantine. The two armies clashed. Constantine drove Maxentius backward, farther and farther, until in his haste to safety, he tried to retreat over the new bridge and fell into his own trap. His horse tumbled off the unstable planking, taking Maxentius in his armor to the bottom of the Tiber, where he drowned.

Maxentius was the last Roman persecutor of the Christians, whom Constantine set free after three hundred years of oppression and death. Constantine so firmly established the rights of Christians to worship God that it would be a thousand years before they would again suffer for their faith.

For three hundred years, the strongest and richest rulers in the world had tried to snuff out Christianity, using force, politics, torture, and death — everything at their disposal. Now all those emperors were gone, while Christ and His Church still stood.

Persecutions Under Julian, A.D. 361

Julian became emperor at the death of his brother Constantius, the son of Constantine the Great. Although Julian had been educated by his father in the Christian faith, he was at heart a pagan, and no sooner was he seated on the throne than he made a public avowal of his belief and trust in the ancient gods of the heathen, earning himself the title Julian the Apostate.

Julian restored idolatrous worship by opening the temples and ordering the magistrates and people to follow his example, but he did not make any laws against Christianity. He allowed every religious sect its freedom, although he exerted all the influence he could to restore the old faith. Although no violent deaths of Christians are recorded as resulting from any orders from Julian, several executions did take place around the empire on orders of heathen governors and officers.

Severus

Venus, the goddess of love, was revered by the Romans, and April was considered the appropriate month to celebrate the triumphs of this goddess. During that month, her temples were thronged with worshipers and her marble statues were decked with flowers. Severus, a Christian centurion in the Roman army, dared to raise his voice against this popular custom, not only refusing to take part in the heathen ceremony, but denouncing Venus herself. Enraged by his words, the crowd seized Severus and dragged him before the judge. He repeated his beliefs firmly in the judge's presence and was condemned to be taken before the temple of Venus to be insulted, stripped, and scourged with a whip called the *plumbetae,* which had lead balls tied at the end of each of its thongs. Severus was beaten by two strong men, delivered over to the public executioners, and beheaded.

Cassian

Cassian was a schoolmaster in a town not far from Rome. When he was arrested for refusing to sacrifice to the idols, his judge decided that his punishment should be entrusted to his students, who didn't like their schoolmaster at all. He was bound and delivered to his students, who fell on him with their styles (the sharp-pointed pieces of iron used to write on wax-covered tablets) and stabbed him to death.

Theodorus, a Christian, was seized and tortured. After being taken from the rack, he was asked how he could endure the pain so patiently. "At first I felt some pain," he replied, "but afterward there appeared to be a young man beside me who wiped the sweat from my face and refreshed me with cold water. I enjoyed it so much that I was sorry to be released."

Marcus

Marcus, the Bishop of Arethusa, a town in Thrace, destroyed a heathen temple and had a Christian church built in its place. This so enraged the heathens of the town that they waited until he was alone and captured him one day. After they had beaten him with sticks, they asked whether he would rebuild the temple he'd torn down. Marcus not only refused to rebuilt it but threatened to destroy it again if anyone else rebuilt it. His persecutors looked around for some way of punishing him, finally deciding on a plan that was as cruel as it was unusual. They tied Marcus with ropes and placed him in a large basket, which they hung in a tree after smearing the poor man's body with honey. After being hung up in the tree, Marcus was asked once more to restore the temple; he refused, and his tormentors left him to die from the stings of the wasps he attracted.

Persecution by the Goths

During the reign of Constantine the Great, the light of the gospel penetrated into the land of the barbarians. In northeastern Europe, which was then called Scythia, some of the Goths were converted, but most of them continued as pagans.

Fritegern, king of the Western Goths, was a friend of the Romans, but Athanaric, king of the Eastern Goths, was at war with them. The Christians living in Fritegern's area lived in peace, but Athanaric, being defeated by the Romans, took out his anger on the Christians in his land.

Sabas was the first to feel the king's anger. He was a humble, modest man, eager to see the Church expand. Athanaric sent out orders that everyone in his land had to sacrifice to the heathen gods and eat the meat that had been offered to the idols. If they refused, they would be put to death. Some of the heathens who had Christian relatives provided them with meat that hadn't been sacrificed to the idols, but Sabas refused to take this way out. He not only refused to comply with the new laws, but publicly said that those who ate the substitute meat were not true Christians.

Sabas was soon arrested and taken before a judge who, seeing he was a poor, unimportant man, had him released. Soon Sabas went to visit Sansala, a Christian missionary; on the third night after his arrival, they were both arrested by a party of soldiers. Sansala was allowed to dress himself and ride, but Sabas was forced to leave his clothing behind and walk. All during the long journey they drove him through thorns and briars, beating him all the way. In the evenings, they stretched him between two beams, fastening his legs to the one and his arms to the other, and left him that way for the night. Even when he was released by a woman who pitied him, Sabas refused to run away.

In the morning, the soldiers tried to persuade both men to renounce their religion and eat the meat that had been consecrated to the idols. They refused, and although Sansala was finally set free, Sabas was drowned.

Nicetas, a Goth living near the Danube with his parents, was a Christian, too. One day Athanaric commanded that an idol should be drawn around on a chariot in all the Christian towns; everyone was ordered to worship the idol when it stopped in front of their house. Nicetas refused to come out when the idol arrived at his house, so the house was set on fire and everyone in it burned to death.

Persecutions by the Vandals, A.D. 429

The Vandals crossed over from Spain to the north coast of Africa and defeated the Roman army there, conquering the whole country under their leader, Genseric. Since the Vandals were of the Arian sect, they abused the Christians wherever they found them, laying waste to all their cities and ruining every beautiful or valuable object they found. They even burned the fields of grain, so anyone escaping their swords would die from famine. They plundered the churches and murdered the bishops and ministers in many cruel ways. Often they poured rancid, filthy oil down the throats of those they captured, drowning them. Others they martyred by stretching their limbs with cords until the veins and sinews burst. Old men found no mercy from them, and even innocent babies felt the rage of their barbarity.

When a town held out against them, the Vandals brought great numbers of Christians to the town walls and killed them, leaving their bodies to rot under the walls until the town had to surrender to escape the plague.

After they took Carthage, the Vandals put the city's bishop and many other Christians into a leaky ship and committed it to the waves, thinking everyone on it would soon die, but the vessel arrived safely at another port. Several Christians were beaten, scourged, and banished to the desert, where God used them to convert many of the Moors to Christianity. Once Genseric discovered this, he sent orders that they and their converts should be tied by the feet to chariots and dragged until they were beaten to pieces.

The Bishop of Urice was burned, and the Bishop of Habensa was banished for refusing to turn over the sacred books. Archinimus, a devout Christian, was brought before Genseric himself for trial. Finding the man firm in his faith, Genseric ordered him beheaded but privately told the executioner, "If the prisoner is courageous and willing to die, don't kill him. I don't want him to have the honor of being a martyr." When the executioner found Archinimus quite willing to die, he returned him to the prison, from which he soon disappeared, probably murdered in secret at the king's order.

Cyrilla, the Arian Bishop of Carthage, was a great enemy to those Christians who professed the pure faith. He persuaded Genseric that he could not allow so many of his subjects to practice their Christianity and enjoy any peace. Genseric first attempted to bribe the Christians away from their faith with promises of worldly gains, but they stood firm, saying, "We acknowledge but one Lord and one faith. You may do whatever you please with our bodies, for it is better we suffer a few temporary pains than endure everlasting misery." Looking for an efficient way to kill so many people at once, the governor finally ordered them all put on a ship filled with wood and straw. The ship was then set on fire, and everyone aboard was either drowned or burned to death. The names of the chief Christians on board the ship were Rusticus, Liberatus, Rogatus, Servus, Septimus, and Boniface.

Telemachus

Rome was celebrating its temporary victory over Alaric the Goth in its usual manner, by watching its gladiators fight to the death in the arena, when suddenly there was an interruption. A rudely clad robed figure boldly leaped down into the arena. Telemachus was one of the hermits who devoted themselves to a holy life of prayer and self-denial and kept themselves apart from the wicked life of Rome. Although few of the Roman citizens followed their example, most of them had great respect for these hermits, and the few who recognized Telemachus knew he had come from the wilds of Asia on a pilgrimage to visit the churches and celebrate Christmas in Rome.

Without hesitating an instant, Telemachus advanced upon two gladiators who were engaged in their life-and-death struggle. Laying a hand on one of them, he sternly reproved him for shedding innocent blood, and then, turning toward the thousands of angry faces around him, called to them: "Do not repay God's mercy in turning away the swords of your enemies by murdering each other!"

Angry shouts drowned out his voice. "This is no place for preaching! On with the combat!" Pushing Telemachus aside, the two gladiators prepared to continue their combat, but Telemachus stepped between them. Enraged at the interference of an outsider with their chosen vocation, the gladiators turned on Telemachus and stabbed him to death.

The crowd fell silent, shocked by the death of this holy man, but his death had not been in vain, for from that day on, no more gladiators ever went into combat in the Colosseûm.

The Spanish Inquisition

The Inquisition of the Church of Rome was, in its days, one of the most terrible engines of tyranny ever created by man. It may be said to date from about the year 1200, when Pope Innocent III sent his inquisitors among the Waldenses and other sects differing from the Church, and continued until

1808. In its course, it totally crushed any Protestants living in Spain: its final count numbered 31,912 people burned alive and 291,450 imprisoned. In the eighteen years that the Dominican monk Thomas of Torquemada led the Inquisition, 10,220 people were burned and 97,322 punished with the loss of property or imprisonment. Although its main victims were citizens of Spain, there were others who became its victims, too.

William Lithgow

William Lithgow was an Englishman born about 1580. Being fond of travel, he was on his way to Alexandria, Egypt, when he was suddenly attacked by nine men, who threw a black cloak over his head and dragged him to the governor's house in Malaga, Spain. There he was accused of being an English spy. Nothing Lithgow could say would convince the local authorities that he was only a tourist passing through the city, so it was decided to torture him until he made his confession. Lithgow was tortured on the rack and then asked if he acknowledged the Pope's supremacy, to which he answered, "You almost murdered me for pretended treason without any grounds. Now you intend to make me a martyr for my religion?"

"You have been arrested as a spy and accused of treachery," his inquisitor replied. "Perhaps you are not a spy, but we have found by your books and writings that you surely are a heretic and therefore deserve even worse punishment than you have received."

They gave Lithgow eight days to consider whether he would convert or not. During this time the inquisitor and others argued frequently with him, to no avail. At last, finding their arguments had no effect and that their threats of torment couldn't shake him, they left Lithgow alone. The eight days were soon over. Lithgow was asked one more time to convert and save his life. "I fear neither death nor fire," he replied. "I am prepared for both, so do your worst!"

That night Lithgow was sentenced to eleven different tortures, and if he did not die from them, he was to be taken to Granada and burned after Easter. The first part of the sentence was carried out with cold-blooded cruelty, but it pleased God to give the poor victim strength of body and mind, and he survived. Then Lithgow waited with resignation for the day that would end his torments.

All of this had been carried out in the strictest of secrecy, since Lithgow was an English subject and not a citizen of Spain, but a servant boy happened to hear the city's mayor discuss Lithgow's case at dinner one night, and he secretly told the story to an English merchant in town named Mr. Wild. Wild told the story to other English merchants living in the town and to the English ambassador at Madrid, Sir Walter Aston, who quickly appealed to the king and council of Spain, obtained an order for Lithgow's immediate release, and put him on board an English warship visiting the city. Two months later, Lithgow arrived safely at Deptford, England, although his left arm remained useless to him for the rest of his life.

Isaac Martin

Isaac Martin, an English trader, was living in Spain with his wife and four children. Because of his first name, the authorities decided Martin must be a Jew and began to harass him to change his religion. In time, Martin decided it would be best if he left the country, but he made the mistake of telling one of his Spanish neighbors his plan and was arrested in the middle of the night.

Brought to his cell in the middle of the night, Martin was told, "You must keep as complete silence here as if you were dead. You must not speak, or whistle, or sing, or make any noise that can be heard. And if you hear anybody cry or make a noise, you must be still and say nothing, under penalty of two hundred lashes."

Martin asked if he was allowed to walk around his cell; the jailer said he was, if he did so very quietly.

All in all, Martin was called to six hearings before his inquisitor on twenty-six trivial, untrue charges. He was promised a lawyer, then told that lawyers were not permitted to speak during a hearing. About a month later, a rope was put around his neck and he was led by it to the altar of the great church. For the crimes of which he stood convicted, the lords of the Holy Office ordered him banished from Spain after receiving two hundred lashes. The next morning the executioner came, stripped Martin to the waist, tied his hands together, and led him out of the prison. He was put on an ass and received his two hundred lashes. After two more weeks in jail, he was sent to Malaga until an English ship arrived to carry him home.

The Inquisition continued until the invasion of Spain by Napoleon Bonaparte in 1808 and the abdication of the throne by Charles IV in favor of his son Ferdinand VII. On February 22, 1813, the Cortes-general of the kingdom assembled in Madrid and decreed that the existence of the Inquisition was no longer in accord with the political constitution that had been adopted by the nation. The bishops and civil courts were returned to their ancient powers and the oppression of the people of Spain finally ended.

3

John Wycliffe

John Wycliffe, who lived during the reign of Edward III in 1371, was the public reader of divinity at the University of Oxford. In a time when few people were educated, he was well known for his scholarship in the fields of philosophy and religion.

At this time Christianity was in a sad state. Although everyone knew the name of Christ, few if any understood His doctrine. Faith, consolation, the use of the law, the works of Christ, our human weakness, the Holy Ghost, the strength of sin, the works of grace, justification by faith, and Christian liberty were never mentioned in the Church.

Instead, the Church was solely concerned with outward ceremony and human traditions. People spent their entire lives heaping up one ceremony after another in hopes of salvation, not knowing it was theirs for the asking. Simple, uneducated people who had no knowledge of Scripture were content to know only what their pastors told them, and these pastors took care to only teach what came from Rome — most of which was for the profit of their own orders, not for the glory of Christ.

Wycliffe, seeing Christ's gospel defiled by the errors and inventions of these bishops and monks, decided to do whatever he could to remedy the situation and teach people the truth. He took great pains to publicly declare that his only intention was to relieve the Church of its idolatry, especially that concerning the sacrament of communion.

This of course aroused the anger of the country's monks and friars, whose orders had grown wealthy through the sale of their ceremonies and from being paid for doing their duties. Soon their priests and bishops took up the outcry, followed by the archbishop, Simon Sudbury, who took away Wycliffe's salary at Oxford and ordered him to stop preaching against the Church. When even that failed, he appealed to the Pope.

Nevertheless, Wycliffe continued speaking his mind to the people in his sermons. King Edward was sympathetic to his preaching, and he also had the support of others of high rank, including John of Gaunt, the Duke of Lancaster, the king's son, and Lord Henry Percy.

The following points, taken from Wycliffe's sermons, summarize his teachings.

- The holy eucharist, after consecration, is not the actual body of Christ.
- The church of Rome is no more important than any other church, and Peter had no more power given to him by Christ than any other apostle.
- The Pope has no more power than any other priest.
- The gospel is enough for any man, without the rules of men, which add nothing to the gospel.
- Neither the Pope nor any other Church official has the power or right to punish transgressors.

In 1377 Wycliffe was ordered to appear before his bishops and answer to their charges, since he had continued to preach on these matters after having been told to stop. He appeared before them on Thursday, February 19, 1377, accompanied by four learned friars, the Duke of Lancaster, and Lord Henry Percy, the Lord Marshal of England.

A great crowd of people had gathered around St. Paul's to see and hear the proceedings, and it took Wycliffe's party a long time to make its way through them to Our Lady's Chapel, where the Church authorities were waiting. In minutes, the Duke of Lancaster and Lord Percy became involved in a heated argument with the bishop over whether Wycliffe should be allowed to sit or must remain standing. Soon arguments gave way to threats, the whole assembly joined in taking sides, and the council had to be dissolved before it was even 9:00 A.M. Wycliffe had escaped punishment for his beliefs.

Soon King Edward III died and his grandson, Richard II, took the throne. The Duke of Lancaster and Lord Percy gave up their government positions and retired to private life, but Wycliffe still enjoyed the support of many noblemen. In 1377, Pope Gregory sent a message to the University of Oxford, rebuking it for allowing Wycliffe's doctrine to take root and demanding he be silenced. This encouraged the Archbishop of Canterbury and other bishops, who decided to meet and agree on what should be done to punish Wycliffe.

On the day Wycliffe was to be examined, a man named Lewis Clifford, who was a member of the prince's court but not a particularly powerful man, strode up to the bishops and sternly warned them not to pass any sentence on Wycliffe. The bishops were so taken aback by his demand that they took no action against Wycliffe that day.

Wycliffe's sect continued to grow despite Church opposition. Some authorities at Oxford attempted to silence him; others gave him whatever support they could; the Church considered him a heretic and threatened his followers with excommunication. For some time Wycliffe was either banished or in hiding, but he returned to his parish of Lutterworth to die in 1384.

In 1415, the synod of Constance declared John Wycliffe a notorious heretic who died in his heresy and ordered his bones removed from consecrated ground. In 1425, Wycliffe was disinterred, his bones burned and thrown into the river. But there is no denying truth, which will even spring up from dust and ashes. Although they burned his bones and drowned his ashes, the Word of God and the truth of John Wycliffe's doctrine would never be destroyed.

Although King Richard allowed himself to be influenced by popes Urban and Boniface IX and published several decrees against the new Protestant doctrines, there is no record of anyone being put to death for holding them during his reign.

Sir William Sautre

Richard II was deposed in 1399 and succeeded by Henry IV. In 1400, during a meeting of parliament at Westminster, Sir William Sautre, a good man and faithful priest, asked permission to speak for the good of the kingdom. The bishops present, suspecting that he wanted to address the subject of religion, convinced parliament that the matter should be referred to the Church convocation, so on February 12, 1400, Thomas Arundel, Archbishop of Canterbury, and his provincial council held a hearing with Sautre.

They charged that he had previously renounced several heretical opinions but continued to teach and preach them. The charges against Sautre, the parish priest of St. Scithe the Virgin in London, were as follows.

- He would not worship the cross on which Christ suffered.

- He would rather worship a temporal king, the bodies of the saints, or a contrite man than the cross.

- He thought it was more important for a priest to teach the Word of God than say the canonical hours.

- He believed that the consecrated bread of communion remains bread and is not physically the body of Christ.

Sautre was given time to prepare an answer to these charges, reappearing before the convocation the following Friday, February 18. He refused to abandon his beliefs and was given one more day to consider his position. Still adamant on the nineteenth, Sautre was ordered stripped of all his Church offices: priest, deacon, subdeacon, acolyte, exorcist, reader, sexton, and even door keeper. Reduced to the state of layman, Sautre was then handed over to the secular legal authorities, and the Church petitioned the king to execute him — something it could not do itself. King Henry readily agreed, becoming the first English king to ever put a heretic to death; Sir William Sautre became the first Englishman to suffer martyrdom in Henry's reign.

After Sautre's death, others who believed as he did took pains to conceal themselves while the unpopular king gathered what support he could by doing the will of the Church, legally condemning the books of Protestantism and making the burning of anyone convicted of heresy legal in England.

John Badby

On March 1, 1409, John Badby, a layman, was examined before Thomas Arundel, the Archbishop of Canterbury, and a number of other lords. The principle charge against him was that he believed the bread was not turned into the actual physical body of Christ upon consecration.

When the examination was finished and all the conclusions were read in English, the archbishop asked Badby if he would renounce his beliefs and adhere to the doctrine of the Catholic faith. He answered that he would stay with his own beliefs. Badby was locked in the friars' mansion, with the archbishop holding the key, until he appeared again on March 15, was declared a heretic and turned over to the secular authorities for punishment.

That afternoon, John Babdy was brought to Smithfield, put in an empty barrel, bound with chains to the stake, and surrounded by dry wood. As he stood there, the king's eldest son happened by and encouraged Badby to save himself while there was still time, but Badby refused to change his opinions. The barrel was put over him and the fire lit.

When Badby felt the fire, he cried, "Mercy, Lord!" and the prince immediately ordered the fire extinguished. Then he promised Badby a yearly stipend from the king if he would return to the faith of the Church. Even then, Badby held his ground to the death.

After Badby's death the bishops, seeking to suppress this doctrine forever and knowing they had a king willing to act on their wishes, drafted a law that condemned the books of heretics and ordered all diocesans to proceed against any heretic with zeal. Death by fire was declared the fate of any heretic who would not recant. After this, the Archbishop of Canterbury issued similarly harsh laws against the Protestants.

With all these laws against them, you would think the Protestants would have been utterly destroyed, and yet such are the works of the Lord that these men multiplied daily instead of being defeated. Their numbers especially increased in London, Lincolnshire, Norfolk, Herefordshire, Shrewsbury, and Calais. Some, however, did recant, among whom were John Purvey, who recanted at Paul's Cross; John Edward, priest of the diocese of Lincoln; Richard Herbert and Emmot Willy, of London; John Becket, of London; John Seynons, of Lincolnshire.

William Thorpe

William Thorpe was a valiant warrior under the banner of Christ. He was examined before the Archbishop of Canterbury in 1407, accused of traveling through England for over twenty years, preaching his reform beliefs to the people.

The archbishop not only demanded that Thorpe deny his beliefs and return to the Catholic Church, but that he turn in anyone he found holding similar beliefs in the future. He was also forbidden to preach until the archbishop was sure he was truly converted.

"Sir," Thorpe replied, "if I agree to this, I would have to be a spy for every bishop in England." Thorpe refused to pledge unconditional submission to the Church. "I will willingly obey God and His law," he said, "and every member of the holy Church that agrees with Christ."

What happened to Thorpe after he was committed to prison isn't known. There is no record of his being burned, so he may have died in prison or secretly escaped.

Poor Christians were being oppressed everywhere, but especially in England at this time, where the king supported the Catholic Church. The Church was so strong there that no one could stand against it; whatever it decreed was obeyed by all men.

John Huss

Richard II had married a native of Bohemia, and through her servants the works of Wycliffe were carried to that country, where they were effectively preached to the people by John Huss of Prague.

Pope John XXIII, seeking to suppress the Bohemians, appointed Cardinal de Columna to look into Huss's preaching and deal with any heresy he might find, so Columna set a date for Huss to appear before him in Rome.

Huss never appeared on the designated date, but King Wenceslaus of Bohemia sent ambassadors to assure Columna that any false doctrine being preached in his country would be taken care of by him, at his expense. At the same time, Huss sent his own ambassadors to assure the cardinal he was innocent of heresy. Columna refused all their pleas and excommunicated Huss for failing to appear in person.

The Bohemians couldn't have cared less about the proclamation of excommunication. The more they grew in knowledge of the Lord through Huss, the less they cared for the Pope and his rules, especially since the Church was divided at that time, with three men arguing over the office of Pope. Although the Bohemian Church officials succeeded in having

Huss banned from Prague, he carried on his work, spreading Wycliffe's message among the people and causing a great uproar over the Church's riches and abuses.

Wenceslaus took advantage of his subjects' state of mind to levy heavy taxes on the clergy, silencing them in Bohemia and filling his treasury at the same time.

In 1414, a general Church conference was held in Constance to resolve the problem of the three popes and also deal with the Bohemians. Assured of safe conduct by both Emperor Sigismund and one of the popes, Huss traveled to the conference, arriving in Constance on November 3. Twenty-six days later, he appeared before the bishops to defend himself, but was not allowed to speak. In violation of the promises made to him, he was imprisoned for "safe keeping" and charged with eight articles of heresy.

On June 7, 1415, Huss was brought before a council and condemned as a heretic when he refused to recant his support of Wycliffe's theology. He was stripped of all his Church offices, made to wear a paper hat with the words *Arch-Heretic* on it, and led past a fire consuming his books.

On July 6, 1415, the hangman stripped Huss of his clothes, tied his hands behind him, then chained his neck to the stake. At that point, Huss told the hangman that he was glad to accept the chain for the Lord's sake. Straw and wood were piled around him to his chin and the fire was lit. As the flames rose around him, Huss was heard to say, over and over, "Jesus Christ, the Son of the living God, have mercy upon me," until the flames choked him. When all the wood was burned, the upper part of his body was still hanging in the chain, so they threw it down, made a new fire, and burned it after cutting his head into small pieces. When he was totally burned, Huss's

ashes were carefully collected and thrown into the Rhone
River.

Jerome of Prague

Upset by the unjust treatment of John Huss, Jerome of
Prague arrived in Constance on April 4, 1415, volunteering to
appear before the council if promised safe conduct. This was
denied him, so Jerome wrote out his thoughts on the council's
treatment of Huss and had them hung on the gates and
porches of Constance's churches and public buildings, then
returned to Bohemia, where he was captured and brought
back to face the council.

Jerome denied that he had done anything against the
Church, answering his accusers firmly and calmly, and was
imprisoned for eleven days, hung by his heels with chains the
whole time. Brought back before the council, he eventually
gave in to their threats to save his life and agreed that John
Huss had been fairly condemned as a heretic. Even then, he
wasn't freed, but returned to prison under slightly better
conditions. It soon became obvious that Jerome had given in
to save his life, not because he had truly changed his mind
about the council, and new articles of heresy were drawn up
against him.

On May 25, 1416, after 340 days of imprisonment, Jerome
was brought before the council of Constance and charged with
107 offenses, all of which he denied or disproved in short
order, silencing his interrogators with his strength and
knowledge of God's law. However, the outcome of the hearing was never really in doubt, no matter what Jerome said.

The Saturday before Ascension Day, Jerome was brought
to hear judgment passed on him. He was given one more

chance to take back his support of John Wycliffe and John Huss, but refused. The council condemned him as a heretic, excommunicated him, and turned him over to the secular authorities.

Jerome went to his death bravely, singing hymns, canticles, and the Doxology, then embracing a drawing of John Huss that he was bound to. Before the fire was lit, he said to the assembled crowd, "What I have just sung, I believe. This creed is my whole faith, but I'm dying today because I refuse to deny that John Huss was a true preacher of the gospel of Jesus Christ."

As the fire flared up around him, Jerome continued his singing, and even when no more sound could be heard from him, his lips continued to move and his head to shake for fifteen minutes. Finally dead in the fire, all his possessions from prison were burned and his ashes were thrown into the Rhone River.

Henry Chicesley succeeded Thomas Arundel as Archbishop of Canterbury, continuing the persecutions. Under him, King Henry VI commissioned John Exeter and Jacolet Germain, the keeper of Colchester Castle, to apprehend William White and others suspected of heresies. Soon after, John Exeter attacked six people in the town of Burgay, Norwich, and sent them to the castle of Norwich.

The old records also show that a great number of people from the towns of Beccles, Ersham, and Ludney were thrown into prison and openly shamed after they recanted. From 1428-1431, about 120 men and women were taken, some only for eating meat on vigil days. Others were handled more cruelly, and some were burned; 78 were forced to recant. Many of the charges against these people were untrue or reported incorrectly by the notaries. Often the simple, uneducated people did not understand the charges brought against them or know how to answer them. Most of them seemed to have been instructed in their faith by William White, a follower of John Wycliffe.

William White

William White, a well-educated, upright, and well-spoken priest, also became a follower of John Wycliffe. He surrendered his priesthood and its salary to marry a godly young woman, but continued to read, write, and preach the doctrines of Wycliffe throughout the Norfolk area, drawing many people to God and developing a reputation as a good, honest man.

His main points of doctrine were:

● That men should seek forgiveness of sins only from God, not priests.

● That the Pope's wicked living made him an enemy of Christ.

● That men should not worship images, other idolatrous paintings, or the saints.

● That the Roman Church brought forth no true doctrine.

● That all monks, friars, and priests were the soldiers of Lucifer and damned.

Brought before Archbishop Henry Chichesley in 1424, White held his ground for some time before being forced to recant. He returned to Norfolk, where he continued to teach and convert the people to the true doctrine of Christ. Captured and tried before William, the bishop of Norwich, he was condemned under thirty articles and burned in September, 1424. After his death, his wife continued his work, bringing even more people to God until she, too, was captured and punished at the hands of the same bishop.

Joan Boughton

On April 28 in the ninth year of Henry VII's reign, an eighty-year-old widow named Joan Boughton was burned at Smithfield for holding eight of Wycliffe's opinions. She held eight of his ten opinions so firmly that all the doctors of London could not make her give up even one of them. Told she would burn for her obstinacy, Mrs. Boughton defied the threat, saying she was so loved by God that she didn't fear the fire.

On January 17, 1497, Richard Milderdale and James Sturdy performed the penance of carrying faggots before the procession of St. Paul's and standing before the preacher during his sermon. The next Sunday, two other men stood at Paul's Cross during the sermon. On Passion Sunday, Hugh Glover bore a faggot before the procession and stood during the sermon, as did four others the following Sunday.

Early in May, 1498, the king had a priest brought before him in Canterbury. Although the priest recanted at the king's demand, he was still burned. Also in 1498, after the beheading of Edward Plantagent, Earl of Warwick, a man named Babram was burned in July; another old man died in Smithfield on July 20.

Jerome Savonarola

Savonarola was an Italian monk, very well educated, who began to preach to the people against the evil living he witnessed within his own order, demanding reforms. As Savonarola's popularity grew, Pope Alexander VI ordered his vicar to proceed with the needed reforms in an attempt to silence the monk, but Savonarola wouldn't be silenced.

When the Pope denounced Savonarola's testimony and ordered him to be silent, the monk finally realized the danger he was in and temporarily stopped preaching. But he took it up again in Florence in 1496 at the request of the people longing for God's Word. Cursed as a heretic, Savonarola told the people that such curses were against true doctrine and should be ignored.

Savonarola was taken from his cloister in 1498, along with two other friars who supported him, and burned as a heretic on May 24, 1499.

4

The State of Religion

By reading this history, a person should be able to see that
the religion of Christ, meant to be spirit and truth, had been
turned into nothing but outward observances, ceremonies,
and idolatry. We had so many saints, so many gods, so many
monasteries, so many pilgrimages. We had too many churches,
too many relics (true and fake), too many untruthful miracles.
Instead of worshiping the only living Lord, we worshiped dead
bones; in place of immortal Christ, we worshiped mortal
bread.

No care was taken about how the people were led, as long
as the priests were fed. Instead of God's Word, man's word
was obeyed; instead of Christ's testament, the Pope's canon.
The law of God was seldom read and never understood, so
Christ's saving work and the effect of man's faith was not
examined. Because of this ignorance, errors and sects crept
into the Church, for there was no foundation for the truth that
Christ willingly died to free us from our sins — not bargaining
with us, but giving *to* us.

Although God allowed His Church to wander for a long
time, at last it pleased Him to restore it to its original foundation. And here we must admire God's wisdom, for just as the
Church fell into ruin because of the ignorance of its teachers,

shortly after the burning of John Huss and Jerome, God gave man the art of printing, which restored knowledge to the Church.

Through the grace of God, men of wisdom were now able to communicate their thoughts accurately and widely, so others could distinguish light from darkness, truth from error, religion from superstition. Knowledge grew in science and in languages, opening a window of light for the world and clearing the way for the reformation of the Church. Still, many were left to suffer before that reform would be complete.

Joan Clerk

In the days of King Henry VII (1506), in the diocese of Lincoln, a faithful woman named Joan Clerk was forced to set fire to her own father, William Tylsworth. At the same time, her husband, John Clerk, did penance by carrying a faggot of wood, as did between twenty-three and sixty others. Those doing penance at Tylsworth's burning were then compelled to wear badges and travel to other towns to do further penance over the space of seven years. Several of them were branded on the cheek for their offenses. One of this group was a rich farmer named Robert Bartlet, whose farm and possessions were taken from him before he was locked in the monastery of Ashryge for seven years.

About the same time, Father Roberts was burned at Buckingham while twenty others carried faggots for penance. Following that, over the course of two or three years, Thomas Bernard and James Mordon were killed and over thirty others were branded on the right cheek for speaking against idolatry and insisting on reading the Scriptures for themselves. Those to be branded were tied to a post by the neck while their hands were held immobile and a hot iron was put to their cheeks.

Thomas Chase

One of those persecuted for the gospel and Word of Christ was Thomas Chase of Amersham, a good man who often spoke against idolatry and superstition. Chase was brought before the blind bishop at Woburn and examined, and although we have no record of his examination, he must have professed Christ's true gospel against idolatry, for he was locked in the bishop's house in Woburn. There he remained in chains, manacles, and irons, all of which he took quietly and faithfully until they lost patience with him and secretly strangled him one day.

There would have been a public uproar if the truth came out about how Thomas Chase had died, so the Church let out a rumor that the good man had hung himself. This would have been impossible, since Chase was chained in such a small area that he could neither sit nor stand, as a woman who saw him dead testified. To be sure no one would be able to examine the body, the authorities buried Chase secretly somewhere near the road between Woburn and Little Marlow.

Laurence Ghest

Laurence Ghest was a tall, good-looking man who had influential friends, which for a time kept the bishops from burning him. Instead, he was locked in prison for two years while they attempted to make him recant his testimony. When he would not recant, a date was set for his burning.

Ghest was a married man with seven children. When he was brought to the stake, the authorities placed his family before him, hoping they could convince him to save his own life at the last minute. His wife begged Ghest to save himself, but he refused, asking her not to stand in his way, for he was running a good race toward salvation. In order to follow Christ, Ghest was forced to renounce not only his own life, but also the family he loved.

A Godly Woman

Of all the people who suffered for Christ and His truth, I know of none as admirable as the godly woman put to death in Chipping Sodbury about this time. Her constancy was glorious to behold, especially when contrasted to the character of the chancellor who condemned her, one Dr. Whittington.

When she was condemned for heresy and brought to the place of execution, a great crowd of people gathered, including Dr. Whittington. This faithful woman persisted in her truthful testimony to the end, committing her cause to the Lord and refusing no pain to keep her conscience clear. Her suffering finally over, the people began to disperse to their homes.

Meanwhile, as the Church was slaughtering this innocent lamb just outside the town, a butcher in town was preparing to slay a bull. Having tied him with ropes, the butcher attempted to hit the bull on the head and kill him, but he missed his killing blow — not being as skilled at killing as the Church's persecutors. The bull, somewhat put out at being hit, broke loose as the people returned from the execution, scattering the townspeople but harming no one until he came to Dr.

Whittington, whom he immediately gored through and killed, to everyone's wonder.

John Browne

John Browne ran into trouble with the Church by sitting too close to a priest on a public barge in 1517.

"Do you know who I am?" the priest demanded. "You're sitting on my clothing!"

"No sir," replied Browne, "I don't know who you are."

"I'm a priest."

"Oh. Are you a parson? a vicar? or a lady's chaplain?"

"No. I'm a soul priest," the man replied. "I sing for a soul."

"Do you? That's wonderful!" Browne exclaimed. "But where do you find this soul when you go to mass?"

"I don't know."

"Ah. And when the mass is done, where do you leave this soul?" continued Browne.

"I don't know."

"But if you don't know where to find or leave this soul, how can you save it?"

"Get out of here!" the priest yelled. "You're a heretic, and I'll get even with you!"

As soon as he left the barge, this priest went directly to Archbishop Warham. Three days later John Browne was taken from his home and imprisoned in Canterbury, where he remained from Low Sunday until the Friday before Whit-Sunday, without his family knowing where he was.

The night before he was to be burned as a heretic, Browne was locked in the stocks at Ashford, Kent, where he lived, and found by his wife, who stayed by his side all night listening to his story. Browne showed her his feet, which had been burned to the bones with hot coals by bishops Warham and Fisher, "to make me deny my Lord, which I will never do. Please, Elizabeth," Browne continued, "do as you have done in the past and bring the children up virtuously in the fear of God."

The next day Browne was burned at the stake, saying, "Into thy hands I commend my spirit. You have redeemed me, O Lord of Truth."

1520-1521

As the light of the gospel began to appear and its number of supporters grew, the bishops became more vehement in their persecutions, causing much suffering in the land. Especially effected were the areas of Buckinghamshire, Amersham, Uxbridge, Henley, and Newbury in the diocese of London, as well as areas in Essex, Colchester, Suffolk, and Norfolk.

It must be understood that this move toward reformation began before the name of Luther was even known. England had always had godly people who were dedicated to the Word of God, sitting up all night reading and hearing and going to great expense to purchase the few books that were available in their tongue. Some would pay as much as a load of hay for a few translated chapters of St. James or St. Paul. Considering the scarcity of books and teachers, it's amazing how the Word of truth spread as far as it did, neighbor teaching neighbor, sharing books and truth and so passing on the knowledge of God.

There were four main areas in which these early reformers disagreed with the Church of Rome:

- They denied the value of pilgrimages.
- They refused to worship the saints.
- They insisted on reading Scripture for themselves.
- They did not believe the physical body of Christ was present in the sacramental bread.

These were simple, honest people who studied and spoke openly of their beliefs, so it was easy for Church examiners to trap them into heretical statements they barely understood and make them implicate others who studied God's Word with them.

In the diocese of Lincoln, bishop John Longland renewed the old persecution by bringing in one or two men who had previously recanted and re-examining them. These implicated others, until a great number of people were brought before the bishop for the crime of assembling together to read the Scriptures. Those who were found to have relapsed were burned; the rest were so burdened with penance that they either died from grief or survived in shame.

King Henry VIII made the bishop of Lincoln's task even easier by ordering all his secular legal authorities to give the bishop any aid and assistance he needed. Now both the law of the land and the law of the Church were against any who studied the Scriptures and upheld their truth.

Martin Luther

Martin Luther, born at Isleben, Saxony, in 1483, was sent to the University of Erfurth. There he entered the convent of the Augustinians and met an old man of his order with whom he discussed many things, especially the remission of sins.

Here he learned the full meaning of Paul's statement, "We are justified with faith." Through his readings of the prophets and apostles and the exercise of faith and prayer, Luther came to believe the truth of Paul's statement and realized the error of what was being taught by the Church's schoolmen. In his four years at Erfurth, Luther also read Augustine, Gabriel, Cameracensis, Occam, Acquinas, Scotus, and Gerson, preferring Augustine above the others.

In 1508, at the age of twenty-six, Luther began teaching and preaching at the University of Wittemberg, impressing many educated men with his scholarship. Three years later he traveled to Rome about a disagreement among the monks and was granted his doctorate at the expense of the Duke of Saxony on his return. Luther soon began to compare the epistle to the Romans and the Psalms, showing people the difference between the law and the gospel. He also argued against the error that said men could earn remission of their sins through works, leading his listeners and readers to God's remission of sins through the love of Jesus, not through indulgences or pilgrimages.

All this time, Luther changed nothing in the ceremonies, carefully observing the rules of his order. The only way he differed from other priests was in stressing the role of faith in the remission of sins.

In 1516, Pope Leo X began selling pardons, by which he gained a large amount of money from people who were eager to save the souls of their loved ones. His collectors assured the people that for every ten shillings they gave, one specified soul would be delivered from the pains of purgatory. The Pope's collector in Germany was a Dominican friar named Tetzel.

On September 30, 1517, Luther put his objections to this practice on the temple adjoining the castle of Wittemberg.

Tetzel immediately called him a heretic, burning his objections and his sermons on indulgences. Luther replied that he was not totally against indulgences, but preferred they be used in moderation.

Soon Maximilian (the German emperor), Charles (the king of Spain), and the Pope contacted Duke Frederick of Saxony and asked him to silence Luther. The duke conferred with many educated men on the problem, including Erasmus, who supported Luther but urged a little more moderation in his writing and preaching. Duke Frederick communicated his concern to Luther but took no action to silence him. The argument continued, but in 1518 Luther wrote to the Pope, totally submitting himself to his authority.

On August 7, 1518, Luther was ordered to appear before the Pope in Rome. The University of Wittemberg and Duke Frederick immediately sent letters back to the Pope requesting that Luther be heard by Cardinal Cajetan in Augsburg. The Pope told Cajetan to call Luther before him in Augsburg and bring him to Rome by force, if necessary.

Early in October, Luther traveled to Augsburg at the request of the cardinal, waiting there three days to receive a promise of safe conduct from the emperor. When Luther came before him, Cajetan rather gently demanded three things of him:

- That he repent and revoke his errors.
- That he promise not to revert back to them.
- That he not do anything that would trouble the Church.

When Luther asked exactly where he had erred, the cardinal showed him Clement's papal bull on indulgences and maintained that faith isn't necessary to someone who receives the sacrament.

In his written reply to the cardinal, Luther stated that the Pope was to be obeyed as long as what he says agrees with the Scriptures, but that the Pope may make mistakes, and any faithful Christian has the right to disagree with him if he is using better reason or better authority for his opinions. He also stated that no one is righteous and that a person receiving the sacrament must believe.

The cardinal told Luther to go away until he was ready to repent. Luther waited for three days in Augsburg, then sent a message to the cardinal that he would keep silent on the pardons if his enemies would do the same. He asked that every other point of conflict be referred to the Pope for his decision. After three more days of waiting, Luther left Augsburg, but before he went, he sent a letter of explanation to the cardinal, along with an appeal to the Pope, which he had published before leaving town.

In January, 1519, Emperor Maximilian died. In October, 1520, he was succeeded by Charles, king of Spain, who received the crown through the efforts of Duke Frederick. In November of that year two cardinals arrived from Pope Leo to see Frederick and make two demands of him: that all Luther's books be burned and that Luther either be killed or sent to Rome. Frederick refused, asking for permission to carry on an investigation by educated men, which would determine if Luther was actually in error. If he were proved wrong and refused to recant, Frederick would no longer protect Luther; until then, he would.

In 1521 Luther attended the diet of Worms at the request of the emperor and with his assurance of safe conduct. The fourth day after he arrived, he was ordered to appear before the emperor and other nobles of the German state, which he did. Told to keep silent until he was asked to speak, Luther was presented with two questions:

- Were the books gathered there his?
- Would he recant them or stand on what he'd written?

Luther replied that the books were his work but asked for time to answer the second question. Brought back the next day, he said it was impossible to categorically defend what he'd written, since he knew he was a fallible man, but he would be willing to be shown where he had made any errors. Asked for a simple yes or no answer to the two questions, Luther said he would stand on what he'd written until proven wrong by the Scriptures.

Unable to move him, the council sent Luther home under his safe-conduct pass. He was kept in hiding for a while, but eventually returned to Wittemberg, where he died at the age of sixty-three after continuing to write and preach for an additional twenty-nine years.

Ulric Zwingle

Ulricus Zuinglius moved to Zurich about 1519, living with the priests in their abbey, observing all their rites and ceremonies for two to three years, and instructing the people in Scripture.

The same year, Pope Leo renewed his pardons throughout the world, but Zwingle opposed them, finding proof in the Scriptures that they were wrong; he also opposed the other corruptions that were currently reigning in the Church. Finally Hugo, the Bishop of Constance, wrote to the senate of Zurich and the college of canons where Zwingle was living, complaining about him and warning everyone to beware of his teachings. Zwingle explained his faith before the senate of Zurich, which wrote back to the bishop in 1522, saying he should restrain the filthy and infamous lives of the priests and do nothing to hinder the liberty of the gospel.

Zwingle himself wrote to the whole Swiss nation. In his letter, he urged them not to oppose the advance of pure doctrine or bring trouble to any priests who had married. Since the Swiss custom was to allow priests their concubines, Zwingle urged them to allow them lawful marriages instead.

Zwingle continued teaching the Word of the Lord for several more years, the Dominican friars preaching against him, until Zwingle offered to debate with them. At this, the judges and senate of Zurich called all the priests in Zurich to a meeting on January 29, 1523, where everyone would be free to speak their minds. The Bishop of Constance sent John Faber as his spokesman. At the close of the meeting, the senate of Zurich declared that the gospel of Christ should be taught out of the Bible and the traditions of men should be abandoned.

Soon the Bishop of Constance wrote to defend the Catholic Church; about June 13, the senate rejected his doctrine and ordered all Catholic images in the city burned. The following April, the city of Zurich suppressed the Catholic mass, replacing it with the Lord's Supper, the reading of the prophets, prayer, and preaching.

Only Zurich took part in this reformation, not the other twelve cities of Switzerland, who remained with the Catholic Church. In December, 1527, a meeting was called in the town of Berne where the two schools of religion were permitted to debate the issues freely. On the Protestant side were Zwingle, Oecolampadius, Bucer, Capito, and Blaurerus. The chief speaker for the Catholics was Conrad Tregerus, and Augustinian friar who tried to prove his points by sources other than the Bible, which was not allowed. Forced to stay within the Bible, Tregerus left the assembly. The arguments continued for nineteen days, with the end result that the city of Berne and those adjoining it abolished the mass, altars, and images of the Catholic Church.

In 1531, the cantons of Zurich and Berne, the only two that had reformed their religion, were insulted by the other five cantons, which led to a war between them. When the five cantons refused to agree to a truce that would allow freedom of religion, Zurich and Berne cut off their roads, starving the cities and forcing them to attack Zurich. Zwingle died in an attempt to reinforce a cut-off garrison of soldiers. His body was mutilated and burned by the Catholic troops. He died at the age of forty-four.

Wendelmuta

In the year 1527, a virtuous widow named Wendelmuta was martyred in Holland. Arrested for her Protestant beliefs, she was imprisoned in Werden Castle until she appeared before the general session of Holland. Several monks were appointed to convince her to recant, but she refused. She also refused the appeals of her family and friends, including a noble lady who was fond of her.

"Wendelmuta," the lady said, "why don't you be quiet and just believe in your heart?"

"You don't know what you're saying," Wendelmuta replied. "It is written, 'With the heart man believeth unto righteousness; and with the mouth confession is made unto salvation.'"

On November 20, she was condemned as a heretic and ordered burned. Coming to the stake, Wendelmuta refused to kiss the cross a monk brought to her. She put a packet of gunpowder to her chest, gave her neck to be bound, and commended herself into God's hands. When the time came for her to be strangled, Wendelmuta closed her eyes and meekly bowed her head. The fire was then set and she was burned to ashes.

The Waldenses

About 1160, Peter Waldo, a citizen of Lyons, suddenly changed his life-style, giving away large amounts of money, studying God's Word, and teaching others how to live virtuous lives. In time, people flocked to him, eager to receive the Scriptures he translated into French and passed out to those who wanted to learn.

Soon the churchmen in the area, who would not explain the Scripture to the people, ordered Waldo to stop his work or face excommunication. Although Waldo ignored their orders, they persecuted his followers so badly that they were all forced to leave the city. The exiled Waldenses dispersed to many places, including Bohemia, Lombardy, and other French provinces. So perfect were they in their knowledge of Scripture that unlettered country men were able to recite the entire book of Job by heart. Others knew the whole New

Testament. One of their fiercest persecutors admitted, "This sect of the Lyonists has a great show of holiness. They live justly before men, believe all good things come from God, and hold all the articles in the creed. Only they blaspheme the Roman Church and hate it."

Everywhere they lived for the next four hundred years, the Waldenses were subject to terrible persecution, especially in the year 1545. Finally, about 1559, the Waldenses living under the Duke of Savoy in the Piedmont area were given freedom to practice their religion without persecution — after generations of patient suffering.

Thomas Bilney

Thomas Bilney was brought up in the University of Cambridge, even as a child studying the liberal sciences and laws. But at last, having found a better teacher in the Holy Spirit, he gave up his study of man's laws to learn the Word of God.

Excited by his love of true religion and godliness, Bilney felt a need to spread the gospel to others. He was quite successful in this, converting, among others, Thomas Arthur and Hugh Latimer. Soon Bilney left the university to travel widely, teach, and preach, accompanied by Thomas Arthur.

Bilney's attacks on the insolence, pomp, and pride of the clergy soon drew the attention of Thomas Wolsey, the cardinal of York, who ordered both Bilney and Arthur imprisoned. On November 27, 1527, Bilney and Arthur were brought before Wolsey and a group of bishops, priests, and lawyers at Westminster.

Asked if he had privately or publicly taught the opinions of Martin Luther or anyone else against the Church, Bilney said that he hadn't. He was then asked if he hadn't previously sworn to actively oppose this type of teaching wherever it was found. Bilney admitted he had sworn to do that, but only under pressure, not legally. Told to recant his errors, Bilney refused, saying he would stand on his conscience; he was declared a heretic.

From December 5–7, Bilney continued to take the position that he had done nothing against Church doctrine and asked permission to call witnesses to that effect. No witnesses were allowed, since he had already been declared a heretic, and on December 7 he was given his last chance to recant before being sentenced. On the advice of his friends, Bilney gave in and was absolved by the bishop. He was sentenced to prison for some time and forced to do penance by going before the procession at St. Paul's bareheaded and carrying a faggot on his shoulder, then stood before the preacher during the sermon.

Returning to Cambridge in 1528, Bilney fell into a deep depression that nothing could lift. His friends stayed with him day and night, afraid that he might kill himself if left alone. This depression stayed with him until 1531, at which time Bilney decided he could no longer deny God's truth, said good-bye to his friends, and left to resume preaching in Norfolk. He urged everyone there to learn from his example and never trust their friends' advice when it came to matters of religion and conscience. He had denied God's truth once to save his life, but never would again.

Bilney was soon arrested and given to the city's sheriffs for execution, one of whom, Thomas Necton, was a close friend. Although Necton was powerless to stop Bilney's execution, he was able to make his waiting more comfortable than normal, even allowing his friends to visit him the night before he died.

Bilney approached the stake in a layman's gown, his arms hanging out, his hair mangled by the Church's ritual divestiture of office. He was given permission to speak to the crowd and told them not to blame the friars present for his death, then said his private prayers.

The officers put reeds and wood around him and lit the fire, which flared up rapidly, deforming Bilney's face as he held up his hands and called out, "Jesus" and "I believe."

Bilney's travel, teaching, and example were very influential at Cambridge, drawing many there to Christ. Among those effected were Hugh Latimer, Doctor Barnes, Doctor Thistel, Master Fooke, Dr. Warner, and Master Soude.

John Tewkesbury

John Tewkesbury was converted by reading Tyndale's Bible and *The Wicked Mammon*. Brought before Cuthbert, the bishop of London, on Wednesday, April 21, 1529, Tewkesbury defended his beliefs for a full week, being so prompt and accurate in his answers that his prosecutors began to fear they were being shamed by a mere leather merchant.

When he was being examined on the errors they said existed in *The Wicked Mammon* (justification by faith), Tewkesbury replied, "Take the book and read it. I don't think you'll find any errors in it."

"I tell you," the bishop said, "that the articles in this book are false, heretical, and condemned by the church. Now what do you say?"

"I don't think there's anything false in the book," Tewkesbury replied, saying he'd studied the gospel for seventeen years and knew the faults in his own soul as well as a mirror showed him the faults on his face. Asked once more to recant his errors, Tewkesbury stated, "I pray that you will reform yourself. If there are any errors in the book, let it be reformed. I think it's fine."

Given a few days to think about it, Tewkesbury gave in to the advice of his friends and recanted, but soon returned to his former stand. Two years later he was apprehended again, brought before Sir Thomas More and the bishop of London, convicted of heresy, and burned at Smithfield on December 20, 1531.

John Frith

Among all the evils of the persecution, none seemed worse to us than the cruel treatment and death of John Frith, a young man who stood far above his companions in knowledge and godliness. Even though his brilliance could have brought him honor and dignity in the secular world, Frith chose to dedicate himself to the Church, believing that the truly good man should live for others, not for himself.

After studying at Cambridge and becoming a very well educated man, Frith became acquainted with William Tyndale, who planted the seed of the gospel and sincere godliness in his heart.

At that time Thomas Wolsey, cardinal of York, built a college in Oxford named Frideswide, now known as Christ's Church — not so much because of his love of learning, but to leave himself a perpetual monument. He gathered together the best vestments, vessels, and ornaments in the land and gave them to the college, also appointing the best professors he could find, one of whom was John Frith. When these professors conferred together about the abuses of the Church, they were all accused of heresy and thrown in prison.

Frith was eventually released on the condition that he stay within ten miles of Oxford, a condition he immediately violated by going abroad for two years. He secretly returned to visit the prior of Reading and was arrested there as a vagabond. Frith was an honest man who found it very difficult to lie convincingly, so the authorities were fairly sure he wasn't a tramp, despite his disguise, but they failed to make him reveal his identity. Until he could be identified, he was locked in the stocks at Reading without food. When he began to suffer badly from hunger, he asked that the local schoolmaster be brought to him.

As soon as Leonard Cox arrived, Frith began to complain of his captivity — in Latin. They talked of many things in both Latin and Greek, then Cox hurried to the town judges and complained of the treatment being given such an excellent, well-educated young man. Frith was freed from the stocks without further punishment.

But he had no time to enjoy his freedom, because Sir Thomas More, then the Chancellor of England, was looking for him all over the country and offering rewards for his capture. Even though he moved from place to place and disguised himself, Frith was eventually captured and imprisoned in the Tower of London.

While there, he and More wrote back and forth to each other, arguing about the sacrament of communion and purgatory. Frith's letters were always moderate, calm, and learned. Where he was not forced to argue, he tended to give in for the sake of peace.

Eventually Frith was taken before the Archbishop of Canterbury, then before the bishop of Winchester, to plead his case. Last of all, he appeared before the assembled bishops in London. His examinations revolved around two points:

purgatory and the substance of the sacrament. As Frith wrote to his friends, "I cannot agree with the divines and other head prelates that it is an article of faith that we must believe — under pain of damnation — that the bread and wine are changed into the body and blood of our Saviour Jesus Christ while their form and shape stay the same. Even if this were true, it should not be an article of faith."

On June 20, 1533, John Frith was brought before the bishops of London, Winchester, and Lincoln and condemned to death. On July 4, he was led to the stake, where he willingly embraced the wood and fire, giving a perfect testimony with his own life. The wind blew the fire away from him, toward Andrew Hewet, who was burning with him, so Frith's death took longer than usual, but he seemed to be happy for his companion and not to care about his own prolonged suffering.

Andrew Hewet

Andrew Hewet was only twenty-four years old, a tailor's apprentice. On one of his days off, he happened to meet William Holt, a noted liar, who decided that he was a Protestant after talking to him for a few minutes. He had Hewet captured and put in irons. Somehow Hewet had a file passed in to him and escaped, only to be recaptured.

At his trial, Hewet was accused of not believing that the consecrated host was the actual body of Christ. Asked what he truly believed, Hewet replied, "As John Frith believes."

"Do you believe it is really the body of Christ, born of the Virgin Mary?" his accusers insisted.

"No."

"Why not?"

"Because," Hewet replied, "Christ commanded me not to believe all men who say, 'Behold, here is Christ, and there is Christ, for many false prophets shall arise.'"

Then the bishops smiled at him, and the bishop of London said, "Frith is a heretic, already sentenced to be burned. Unless you revoke your opinion, you will burn with him."

"Good."

Asked again if he would change his mind, Hewet said he would do as Frith did. On July 4, 1533, Andrew Hewet was burned with John Frith.

Thomas Bennet

Thomas Bennet was born in Cambridge and made a master of arts there. The more he grew in the knowledge of God and His holy Word, the more he came to abhor the time's corrupt state of religion until, hoping to live with more freedom of conscience, he left the university and moved to Exeter in 1524, where he became a teacher.

Bennet was a quiet man whose greatest pleasure was attending sermons. In his spare time, he studied the Scripture privately, not sharing his views with anyone until he was sure they felt as he did. But every tree and herb has its due time for bringing forth fruit; so did Bennet. Seeing the glory of God blasphemed, idolatrous religion maintained, and the power of the Pope extolled, he finally decided he had to speak out, even though he knew he would be punished. In October, he fastened to the doors of the cathedral a scroll that said, "The Pope is antichrist, and we ought to worship God only, not saints."

As soon as the message was found, the authorities attempted to find the heretic who had posted it. Bennet quietly went about his life, attending services and teaching his students while Church and secular authorities looked for the culprit. But Bennet was such a quiet, faithful man that no one would ever suspect him of doing such a bold, dangerous thing.

After a while, when it had no success finding the heretic, the Church decided to publicly curse him or her with book, bell, and candle — considered in those days to be the most terrible curse of all. Bennet sat in the congregation and heard himself excommunicated, given over to the devil, and deprived of the benefits of the Church's pardon for his sins. All the powers of the corrupted Church were invoked against him: the saints, the Pope, the monks and friars — everything that Bennet considered worthless, anyway.

The congregation was sitting silently, awed by this display of the Church's wrath and hoping none of it fell on them by mistake, when Bennet, suddenly seeing the irony of the situation, began to laugh. Once started, he couldn't seem to stop, and he was apprehended as the heretic the Church was damning so theatrically. When his friends later asked him why he'd betrayed himself by laughing in church, Bennet replied, "Who could keep from laughing at their little conceits and interludes?" At his trial, he confessed, "It was I that put up those bills, and I would do it again, for what I wrote is true."

At his execution, Bennet exhorted the people to worship and know the true God, forsaking the devices, fantasies, and imaginations of the Church. Most of the people there, including the scribe who wrote his death sentence, were convinced that Bennet was a good man and a servant of God.

William Tyndale

William Tyndale was born near the border of Wales and brought up in the University of Oxford, where he studied languages, the liberal arts, and the Scriptures. After further study at Cambridge, he became the tutor of the children of Lord Welch, a nobleman of Gloucestershire.

Abbots, deans, archdeacons, and other well-educated men often visited Lord Welch to discuss the works of Luther and Erasmus, as well as questions of Scripture. Whenever he disagreed with their positions — which was often — Tyndale never hesitated to defend his opinion with Scripture. One evening, Lord and Lady Welch returned from a dinner and told Tyndale about the discussion that had taken place there. Tyndale began to explain that what they'd heard was wrong, but was cut short by Lady Welch. "There was a doctor there who could afford to spend a hundred pounds. Another could easily spend two hundred, and a third, three hundred. Why should we believe you instead of them?"

At the time, Tyndale was translating Erasmus's *The Manual of a Christian Soldier.* When it was done, he gave a copy to Lord and Lady Welch. Once they read the book, they entertained the churchmen far less frequently.

Soon the area priests began to complain about Tyndale in the pubs and other places, saying his works were heresy and adding to what he said to make their accusation appear true. Tyndale was called before the bishop's chancellor, threatened, and charged with many things, but he was allowed to leave unharmed.

After this, Tyndale decided he'd better leave the area, so he traveled to London, hoping to secure a place with Cuthbert

Tonstal, the bishop of London. When he was unable to do that, he left for Germany.

Tyndale, partly though the influence of John Frith, had decided that the people needed to be able to read Scripture for themselves, instead of trusting the Church to explain it to them honestly and fully. He believed that the corruption of the Church was tolerated only because people didn't know any better — and the Church wasn't about to teach them any better, or its excesses and privileges would be in danger.

In 1526, Tyndale published his English translation of the New Testament and began on the Old Testament, adding prologues to each book. In addition, he published *The Wicked Mammon* and *The Practice of Prelates,* sending copies to England.

After traveling to Germany and Saxony, where he met with Luther and other learned men, he finally settled in Antwerp, The Netherlands.

When his books — especially the New Testament — began to be widely read in England, the bishops and prelates of the Church did everything in their power to condemn them and point out their "errors." In 1527, they convinced the king to ban all Tyndale's works in England.

Meanwhile, Cuthbert Tonstal, the bishop of London, worked with Sir Thomas More to find a way to keep the translations out of the public's hands. He became acquainted with Augustine Packington, an English merchant who secretly supported Tyndale, and Packington promised the bishop that he would deliver every copy of the translation's next edition, if the bishop supplied the funds for the purchase. When the bishop agreed, Packington explained the deal to Tyndale. Soon the bishop of London had his books, Packington his praise, and Tyndale all the money, part of which he promptly used to print a new edition that he shipped into the country. The rest of the money supported Tyndale for a while.

Tonstal publicly burned all the copies he had bought, an act that offended the people so much that the Church promised it would provide its own error-free translation. Nothing was done to fulfill this promise. In fact, in May 1530 the Church declared that such a translation was unnecessary, which immediately increased the sale of Tyndale's work.

Tyndale was eventually captured by the emperor in Antwerp, his books were all seized, and he was imprisoned for a year and a half before being condemned under the emperor's decree of Augsburgh. He was tied to the stake, strangled, and burned in Vilvorden in 1536, dying with these words: "Lord! Open the King of England's eyes!"

John Lambert

John Lambert, who was converted by Bilney, fled the persecutions of the time by going abroad, where he joined Tyndale and Frith and served as chaplain for the British living in Antwerp. After a little over a year, he was captured in 1532 and brought to London to answer forty-five charges before Warham, the Archbishop of Canterbury, but the archbishop died in August, 1532, and Lambert was set free.

This was during the reign of Henry VIII, shortly after the destruction of England's monasteries and Henry's divorce from Queen Catherine and remarriage, a time when supporters of the gospel were generally safe in their beliefs.

On his release, Lambert returned to London as an instructor of Greek and Latin. In 1538, he was present at a sermon preached in St. Peter's Church by Dr. Taylor, a Protestant who would later become the bishop of Lincoln and die under

Queen Mary. When the sermon was over, Lambert approached Taylor to disagree with him on the matter of the sacrament.

In an effort to satisfy Lambert, Taylor discussed the matter with Dr. Barnes. Now Dr. Barnes was in favor of preaching the gospel, but he thought bringing this issue up would only hinder the spread of the gospel at that time, so he suggested Taylor talk to Archbishop Cranmer.

What had started as a private conversation was rapidly becoming a public matter. Cranmer hadn't yet changed his mind on the sacrament — although he would later — so he called Lambert into open court to defend his case. Although we don't know what went on in the meeting, rumors about their disagreement spread throughout the whole court.

The bishop of Winchester was one Stephen Gardiner, counsellor to the king — a cruel, crafty man who was always looking for a way to hinder the gospel. He went to King Henry and told him he was hated by the people for several reasons: for destroying the monasteries, abolishing the Pope's authority, and divorcing his wife. But if the king showed the people that heretics would still be punished, Gardiner said, Henry would regain his popularity with the people. The king immediately agreed, saying he would personally judge every heretic in the land.

Lambert was brought from prison under guard to be judged by Henry, with all the nobles and bishops in attendance. Given permission to speak, Lambert said that he was glad the king was willing to hear religious controversies, especially since he was a king with such judgment and knowledge.

"I didn't come here," Henry interrupted brusquely, "to hear my own praises! Go straight to the matter."

Taken aback by the king's harsh words, Lambert was silent.

"Why are you just standing there?" Henry demanded. "In the sacrament of the altar, do you say it's Christ's body or not?"

"I agree with St. Augustine. It is the body of Christ in certain ways," Lambert answered.

"Don't answer me from St. Augustine or anyone else. What do *you* say?" Henry was addressing Lambert in Latin.

"Then I deny it's the body of Christ."

Henry then turned the interrogation over to Cranmer, who, along with the bishop of Winchester and Tonstal, the bishop of Durham, attempted to change Lambert's mind.

Lambert was overwhelmed. Besieged by taunts and threats from men of power, amazed at the majesty of the place and the king's presence, and exhausted from standing for five hours, he lapsed into silence.

Finally the day was over. King Henry turned to Lambert once more. "What do you say now, after all the instruction of these learned men? Are you satisfied? Will you live or die? What do you say? Take your choice."

Lambert answered, "I yield and submit myself wholly into your hands."

"Commit yourself into God's hands, not mine," was the reply.

"I commend my soul into God's hands, but my body I yield to your clemency.

"If you commit yourself to my judgment, you will die," Henry replied. "I will not be a patron to heretics." The king turned to Cromwell, the chief friend of the Protestants. "Cromwell, read the sentence of condemnation against him."

Through the advice of the bishop of Winchester, Satan had Lambert condemned by his fellow Protestants — Taylor, Barnes, Cranmer, and Cromwell — all of whom would later suffer for the gospel's sake. Of all the people burned at Smithfield, none were handled as cruelly as Lambert, yet in the midst of his torments, lifting up his mangled, burning hands, he cried to the people, "None but Christ. None but Christ!"

5

Robert Barnes

On his graduation from the University of Louvain, Robert Barnes was made prior and master of the Augustines at Cambridge. At that time little literature was taught at Cambridge, but Barnes introduced its study and produced many educated young men who were familiar with the works of Terence, Plautus, Cicero, and others. Once literature was established, Barnes began teaching Paul's epistles, producing many good men for the Church.

Through his reading, discussions, and preaching, Barnes became famous for his knowledge of Scripture, always preaching against bishops and hypocrites, yet he continued to support the Church's idolatry until he was converted to Christ by Bilney.

Barnes preached his first sermon as a Protestant at St. Edward's Church in Cambridge and was immediately accused of heresy. Brought before Cardinal Wolsey, his friends convinced Barnes to abjure, and he did public penance at St. Paul's before being imprisoned for a year and a half. On his release from prison, Barnes was sent as a freed prisoner to the Austin friars in London, but they soon brought more charges on him, and he was forced to flee to Luther in Antwerp.

While in Antwerp, Barnes became friends with Luther, Melancthon, the Duke of Saxony, and the King of Denmark, who sent him with the Lubecks as an ambassador to Henry VIII. Sir Thomas More wanted to capture Barnes while he was in the country, but the king wouldn't allow him to, since Cromwell, his friend and advisor, had become the protector of the Protestants. Barnes was allowed to dispute with the bishops and leave the country at will. He returned to Luther at Wittemberg to publish his books, then went back to England at the beginning of Queen Anne Boleyn's reign, becoming a well-respected preacher.

Once Stephen Gardiner arrived from France, trouble fell on the Protestants again. From then on, religion suffered, as did Queen Anne and Cromwell, and Barnes was imprisoned in the Tower of London until he was burned on July 30, two days after Cromwell's death. Two other Protestants were burned with him — Gerrand and Jerome — plus three Catholics — Powel, Featherstone, and Abel. Seeing both Protestant and Catholic being punished for their faith at the same time confused the whole nation, although it was the political result of a division of the king's council, half of whom were Catholic, half Protestant.

The Law of the Six Articles

In 1539, at the instigation of Henry VIII, parliament passed the Six Articles upholding the Catholic doctrines of priestly celibacy and transubstantiation. The punishment for breaking this law was death, with no provision for recantation, although this was softened a bit by parliament in 1544, which made provision for recantation and penance for the first two convictions and required death for the third offense.

At the same time, parliament banned all of Tyndale's books and all songs, plays, and books in English that violated the Six Articles. The text of the Bible was forbidden to all women, craftsmen, apprentices, journeymen, servants, yeomen, farmers, and laborers. Noblemen and their wives were allowed to read the Bible if they did so quietly and didn't expound upon it.

Another provision of the Law of the Six Articles allowed a person accused of heresy to bring forward witnesses on his behalf, in equal or greater number of witnesses being called against him. This had never been allowed before in heresy trials.

Kerby and Clarke

Kerby and Clarke were captured in Ipswich in 1546 and brought before Lord Wentworth and other commissioners for their examination. At that time they were asked if they believed in transubstantiation. Admitting they did not, both stated their belief that Christ had instituted the Last Supper as a remembrance of His death for the remission of sins, but there was no actual flesh or blood involved in the sacrament.

Kerby was sentenced to burn in Ipswich the next day; Clarke the following Monday in Bury. When he heard his sentence, Kerby bowed devotedly, raised his hands, and proclaimed, "Praised be Almighty God!"

The next day Kerby was brought to the marketplace at ten in the morning, where the stake, wood, and straw were in place. He removed his clothing to his shirt, still in his nightcap, and was fastened to the stake with irons. Approximately two thousand people were present, including Lord Wentworth. After a sermon by Dr. Rugham, during which Kerby commented to the assembled crowd whenever he agreed or disagreed with Rugham, he was given time to say his prayers, which moved everyone, including Lord Wentworth, to tears. The fire was lit and Kerby called to God, knocking on his breast and holding his hands up as long as he could. Everyone present praised God for Kerby's faithfulness to the end.

As Roger Clarke was being brought to the stake the next Monday in Bury, a procession of the host met them. Clarke refused to bow or remove his cap to the procession, vehemently rebuking such idolatry and angering the officers around him.

The Death of Henry VIII

After a long illness, toward the end of January, 1547, it became obvious to King Henry's doctors that he was dying. Although they felt he should know the state of his health, no one was willing to risk telling him. The task fell on one Master Denny, who boldly told Henry that he was dying and urged him to prepare for it by calling on God in Christ for grace and mercy.

The king listened to Denny and considered his sins, which he regretted, yet concluded that "the mercy of Christ is able to pardon me all my sins, even if they were worse than they are."

Glad to hear Henry thinking this way, Denny asked if he would like to speak to anyone. Henry replied that he would like to see Dr. Cranmer, but by the time Cranmer arrived, Henry was unable to speak and barely conscious. He was able to reach out and grasp Cranmer's hand, however. Cranmer urged the king to put his trust in Christ and call on His mercy, and Henry pressed Cranmer's hand as a sign that he was doing so, then died. Henry had ruled for thirty-seven years and nine months, leaving behind three children — Edward, Mary, and Elizabeth.

Patrick Hamilton

The first Scottish martyr was Patrick Hamilton, Abbot of Ferne, the son of Sir Patrick Hamilton of Kincavil and Catherine Stewart, a daughter of the Duke of Albany. Young Hamilton was educated at St. Andrews in the liberal philosophy of John Mair, then read Luther for himself. He was always noted for having a liberal mind and adopted Protestant theology wholeheartedly, but fled to Wittemberg when he was called to appear before an ecclesiastical council.

There Hamilton became friendly with Luther and Melancthon, who recommended him to Lambert, the head of the University of Marpurg. Lambert instructed Hamilton even more fully in Protestantism, which produced a great change in him. Where before he had been skeptical and timid, he now became courageous, almost rash, and decided to return to Scotland and preach the faith there.

He arrived back in Scotland in 1527 and publicly addressed the people for a time before being arrested and imprisoned. His youth — he was only twenty-eight — his talent, and his pleasant, gentle disposition made many churchmen try to change Hamilton's mind, or at least convince him to stop preaching his beliefs and disturbing the Church. Hamilton held so firm that he converted a Catholic priest named Aless who visited his cell. In time, Aless suffered persecution for his new faith and was burned.

On the scaffold, Hamilton gave his servant all his clothing, comforting him by saying, "What I am about to suffer, dear friend, appears fearful and bitter to the flesh. But remember, it is the entrance to everlasting life, which none shall possess who deny their Lord." Even though his executioner's lack of skill prolonged Hamilton's suffering, he never ceased preaching to those standing near him. "How long, O God," he exclaimed, "shall darkness cover this kingdom? How long will You allow this tyranny of men?" He died with the words "Lord Jesus, receive my spirit" on his lips.

Henry Forrest

A few years after Patrick Hamilton's death, Henry Forrest preached that Hamilton was a martyr and what he'd proclaimed was true. He was put in prison by James Beaton, the Archbishop of St. Andrews, who sent a friar named Walter Land to hear Forrest's confession. In his supposedly secret confession, Forrest affirmed his belief in Hamilton and all he had died for. The friar immediately went to the bishop and told him everything Forrest had confessed, which was used as evidence in his trial.

On the day of his execution, Forrest was stripped of his Church offices in front of the clergy, calling out, "Fie on falsehood! Fie on false friars! Revealers of confession! After this day let no man ever trust any friars, condemners of God's Word and deceivers of men!" He suffered death for his faithful testimony at the north church stile at St. Andrews.

James Hamilton, Catherine Hamilton, Straiton, Gourlay

In 1534, James Hamilton, Catherine Hamilton, David Straiton, and Norman Gourlay were called before King James V in Edinburgh. James Hamilton had been accused by the Church of holding the opinions of his brother Patrick. King James warned Hamilton not to appear at his trial, where he wouldn't be able to help him, but to leave the country and forfeit his lands and property to save his life.

Catherine Hamilton, James's sister and King James's aunt, was charged with not believing she could be saved by works. After a long discussion with a lawyer named John Spens, she concluded, "Work here, work there! What kind of working is all this? I know perfectly that no kind of work can save me except the works of Christ, my Lord and Savior!"

The king turned aside and laughed at her reply, then called her up to him and convinced her to recant for the sake of the family. She was set free.

Straiton was a gentleman from a good family, but he quarreled with the Bishop of Moray over his tithes. One day when he was challenged by the Church collectors, Straiton ordered his servants to throw every tenth fish they caught back into the sea and told the collector to go look for his tax there. After this, he calmed down and became a sincere convert of the Reformation. Accused of heresy, Straiton refused to recant and was burned with Gourlay on August 27, 1534.

Dean Thomas Forrest

Every Sunday, Dean Thomas Forrest preached from the gospel, something that was normally only done by the friars. In retaliation, the friars accused him of showing the mysteries of Scripture to the common people, reading the Bible in the common tongue, and making the clergy detestable in the sight of the people.

The Bishop of Dunkeld called in Dean Thomas and advised him not to preach to the people every Sunday. If he wanted to do that, he should become a friar.

Dean Thomas replied that preaching from the gospel once a week was barely enough, but the bishop maintained that they were not ordained to preach, admitting that even he didn't know the Old and New Testaments himself, being content to know his mass book and pontifical. At this time, nothing was done to Dean Thomas, even though he stood his ground and refused to stop preaching the Bible.

Shortly afterward, Dean Thomas was arrested, along with two friars named Keillor and Beveridge, a priest named Duncan Simpson, a gentleman named Robert Forrester, and three or four others from the town of Stirling. Accused of being chief heretics and teachers of heresy, none of them were given the opportunity to recant. The main charges against them were that they were present at the marriage of a priest and ate meat at the wedding, which was held during Lent. In February of 1538 or 1539, they were all burned in Edinburgh.

George Wishart

In 1543, George Wishart was teaching at the University of Cambridge. He was a tall man, slightly sad-looking, with black hair and a long beard. A pleasant man, this native of Scotland was polite and humble, a man who loved to travel, learn, and teach. He dressed simply in black and regularly gave his used clothing to the poor.

Wishart was noted for his Christian charity and spartan style of living, eating only two meals a day and fasting one day out of four. He slept on a straw mattress under canvas sheets that he gave away whenever he changed his bed.

Wishart had been arrested and imprisoned in the castle of St. Andrew, locked in chains for his doctrine. On the day he was summoned to appear before the cardinal at St. Andrews, he was escorted to the church by one hundred armed men. Pausing momentarily to hand his purse to a poor man lying by the door, he was then escorted to the cardinal. Dean John Winryme stood in the pulpit to deliver a sermon on heresy, then Wishart stood by the pulpit and heard John Lauder read the charges against him.

When this well-fed priest had read them all, his face running with sweat and frothing at the mouth like a boar, he spit in Master George's face and demanded, "What do you say to these accusations, you traitor and thief?"

Master George briefly knelt down in the pulpit to pray, then answered calmly and politely, requesting that they allow him to explain his doctrine for three reasons.

"The first is because through preaching the Word of God, His glory is made manifest. It is reasonable, therefore, for the advancing of the glory of God, that you hear me teaching the pure Word of God.

"Secondly, since your salvation comes from the Word of God, it would be unrighteous of you not to hear me teach the Word of God.

"Third, your doctrine is full of blasphemous and abominable words coming from the devil. You should know my doctrine so I don't die unjustly to the peril of your own souls.

"Since I came to this country, I taught nothing but the commandments of God, the twelve articles of the creed, and the Lord's Prayer in the mother tongue. In Dundee, I taught the epistle of Paul to the Romans. And I will show you how I taught...."

His accuser suddenly shouted, "You heretic, traitor, and thief! It wasn't legal for you to preach! You took that power into your own hands without authority from the Church."

The assembled prelates exclaimed, "If we allow him to preach here, he is so crafty and knowledgeable of the Scriptures that he'll turn the people against us."

Master George, seeing what they were planning, asked to appeal his case to the lord governor, since he was arrested by him in the first place and should be judged by his legal authorities, not the Church.

Despite his appeal, eighteen articles of heresy were read against Wishart, each of which he answered with Scripture that soundly supported his doctrine. When the bishops were through, they condemned Wishart to burn as a heretic, ignoring all his replies, and told the congregation to leave.

Returned to prison in the castle, Wishart refused to make his confession to the two friars who arrived, demanding Dean John Winryme, who had preached at his hearing, instead.

The fire was made ready and the gallows erected. The cardinal, afraid Wishart would be freed by his friends, ordered all the castle's arms aimed at the gallows. Wishart's hands were tied behind him and he was led to the fire with a rope around his neck and a chain of iron around his waist.

He told the assembled crowd not to let his death turn them from the Word of God. "I exhort you to love the Word of God and suffer patiently, with a comfortable heart, for the sake of the Word, which is your salvation and everlasting comfort." Then he asked the crowd to help his followers remain firm in his teaching. "I don't fear this grim fire. If any persecution comes to you for the Word's sake, don't fear those who kill the body but cannot kill the soul. Tonight I will dine with the Lord."

After Wishart asked God to forgive those who condemned him, the hangman kneeled before him. "Sir, please forgive me. I am not guilty of your death."

"Come here," Wishart replied. When the hangman went to him, Wishart kissed his cheek and said, "There's a token of my forgiveness. Do your job." As Wishart was hung and burned, the crowd mourned and complained that an innocent lamb had been slaughtered.

Adam Wallace

Adam Wallace was tried in the Blackfriars' church in Edinburgh before a large panel of priests, bishops, archbishops, professors, and civil authorities. His accuser was John Lauder, parson of Marbottle, clad in a surplice and red hood.

Wallace looked like a simple, poor man when he was brought in.

Lauder began: "Adam Wallace, you are accused of the following heresies. First, you have taught that the bread and wine on the altar are not the body and blood of Christ after consecration."

Wallace turned to the panel of judges. "I never taught or said anything but what I found in this book, which is the Word of God. If I was wrong, I will accept your punishment, but everything I said is from this book." Then he quoted Matthew 26:26–28 and Luke 22:19.

The charge was read again, and Wallace was told to answer yes or no to it. "I only taught those who asked me to, and even then, not very often. What I said was that if the sacrament were truly administered and used as the Son of the living God instituted it, God was there."

Asked the same question once more, Wallace used Scripture to show why he did not believe the host could possibly be the physical body and blood of Christ.

The accuser went on to the second article. "You taught that the mass is idolatry, hated by God."

Wallace replied, "I've read the Word of God in three languages, yet I never once saw the word *mass* in it. If the mass is not founded on the Word, it's idolatry, which God hates. But if someone can show me the word in Scripture, I'll admit that I'm wrong and submit to correction and punishment."

The accuser continued. "You openly taught that God is just bread, sown of corn, grown in the earth, and baked by men. Nothing more."

"I worship the Father, the Son, and the Holy Ghost, three persons in one Godhead, who made and fashioned the heaven and earth and all in it. I don't know what God you worship, but if you show him to me, I'll be able to tell you what he is."

Wallace remained firm in his testimony, was sentenced, and returned to prison. On the day of his death, his guards warned him not to speak to the crowd, but many people said, "God have mercy on you" as he passed, to which he replied, "And on you, too." At the stake, he said to the crowd, "Don't be offended by my dying for the truth's sake. The disciple is not greater than his Master." The guards threatened him for speaking, so Wallace looked up to heaven. "They will not let me speak." The fire was lit, and Adam Wallace went faithfully to God.

Walter Milne

Among the martyrs of Scotland, Walter Milne was pivotal, for out of his ashes sprang thousands of others holding the same opinions, which forced the Church of Scotland to debate true religion with the French and the Catholic Church.

Milne was a parish priest of Lunan who embraced the doctrines of the Reformation and was condemned in the time of Beaton. He was able to escape safely from prison and hid in the country of Scotland until the leniency of the queen dowager allowed him to resume his preaching. Forced into hiding a second time, he was captured and tried for heresy at St. Andrews at the age of eighty-two.

The following dialogue took place between Milne and Andrew Oliphant, one of the bishop's priests, at his April 1551 trial.

"What do you think of priests marrying?" Oliphant asked Milne.

"I hold it a blessed bond; for Christ Himself maintained it, approved of it, and made it available for all men. But you don't think it's available for you. You abhor it while taking other men's wives and daughters, not respecting the bond God made. You vow chastity and break it. St. Paul would rather marry than burn, which I have done, for God never forbid marriage to any man."

"You say there are not seven sacraments."

"Give me the Lord's Supper and Baptism, and you can divide the rest among yourselves. If there are seven, why have you omitted one of them — marriage — and given yourself to immorality?"

"You are against the sacrament of the altar. You say the mass is idolatry."

"A lord or a king calls many to a dinner, then when the hall is ready he rings a bell to summon the crowd, turns his back on his guests, eats alone, and mocks them. This is what you do, too."

"You deny the sacrament of the altar is the actual body of Christ."

"The Scripture of God is not to be taken carnally, but spiritually, and stands in faith only. As far as the mass, it is wrong. Christ was offered once on the cross for man's sins and will never be offered again. He ended all sacrifice."

"You deny the office of bishop."

"Those you call bishops don't do a bishop's work as defined by Paul's letter to Timothy. They live for sensual pleasure and don't care for their flock. They don't honor the Word of God, but seek honor for themselves."

"You speak against pilgrimages."

"They are not commanded in Scripture. There is no greater immorality committed in any place than at your pilgrimages."

"You preach secretly in houses and openly in the fields."

"Yes. And on the sea, too, in a ship."

"Will you recant? If not, I will sentence you."

"I am accused of my life. I know I must die once and therefore, as Christ said to Judas, what thou doest, do quickly. I will not recant the truth. A am corn, not chaff; I will not be blown away with the wind or burst by the flail. I will survive both."

Andrew Oliphant ordered Milne given to a secular judge to be burned as a heretic, but the provost of the town, Patrick Learmont, refused to be Milne's secular judge, as did the bishop's chamberlain. The whole town was so offended at the sentence that they wouldn't even sell the bishop's servants a rope for tying Milne to the state or a tar barrel. Finally Alexander Summerwail, more ignorant and cruel than the rest, acted as a secular judge and sent Milne to the stake.

When Milne was brought to be executed, Oliphant ordered him to climb up to the stake. "No," Milne repled. "You put me up there and take part in my death. I am forbidden by God's law from killing myself. But I go up gladly."

Oliphant put the old man up himself.

Then Milne addressed the crowd. "Dear friends, I suffer today for the defense of the faith of Jesus Christ, set forth in the Old and New Testaments. I praise God that He has called me to seal up His truth with my life, which, as I have received it from Him, I willingly offer to His glory. If you would escape eternal death, do not be seduced by the lies of priests, monks, friars, priors, abbots, bishops, and the rest of the sect of antichrist. Depend only on Jesus Christ and His mercy to save you."

There was great mourning and crying among the crowd as Milne died, and their hearts were so inflamed by his death that he was the last religious martyr to die in Scotland.

6

John Rogers

John Rogers was educated at the University of Cambridge, then served as chaplain to the English merchants living in Antwerp, The Netherlands. There he met William Tyndale and Miles Coverdale, both of whom had previously fled England. Converted to Protestantism, Rogers aided the two in translating the Bible into English, married, and moved to Wittemberg, where he was given a congregation of his own.

Rogers served his congregation for many years before returning to England during the reign of King Edward VI, who had banished Catholicism and made Protestantism the state religion. He served in St. Paul's until Queen Mary took the throne, banished the gospel, and brought Catholicism back to England.

Even then, Rogers continued to preach against the queen's proclamation until the council ordered him to remain under house arrest in his own home, which he did, even though he could easily have left the country. Protestantism was not going to flourish under Queen Mary; Rogers knew he could find work in Germany; and he did have a wife and ten children to think of, but he refused to abandon his cause to save his life. He remained a prisoner in his own house for a long time, but eventually Bonner, Bishop of London, had Rogers imprisoned in Newgate with thieves and murderers and Winchester condemned him to death.

Early on the morning of Monday, February 4, 1555, the jailer's wife woke Rogers and told him to hurry and dress; this was the day he was to burn. His wife and eleven children met him on the way to Smithfield, but Rogers still refused to recant. Arriving at Smithfield, he was given one more chance by Sheriff Woodroofe.

"That which I have preached I will seal with my blood," Rogers replied.

"Then," said Woodroofe, "you are a heretic."

"That will be known on the day of judgment."

"Well, I'll never pray for you!"

"But I will pray for you."

A little before the burning, a pardon arrived, but Rogers refused to recant and accept it, becoming the first martyr to suffer death during the reign of Queen Mary.

Lawrence Sanders

After Queen Mary prohibited Protestant preaching in the first year of her reign, several ministers continued to preach the gospel as private pastors. One of these was Lawrence Sanders.

Sanders, from a prosperous noble family, studied at Eton and King's College, Cambridge. His widowed mother wanted him to become a merchant, so he apprenticed himself to a merchant named Sir William Chester. But soon Sanders realized that he really wanted to be a preacher, and his master, who was a good man, set him free from his contract so Sanders could return to Cambridge as a divinity student.

Sanders began to preach during the reign of King Edward, when Protestantism became the official religion of England. After holding several positions, he became a preacher in the countryside of Leicestershire, where he taught diligently until being offered a church in London named Allhallows. Just as he was about to give up his position in the country to concentrate on his London parish, Queen Mary made her bid for the throne. Seeing that Mary would bring hard times on all Protestants, Sanders kept both positions. If he had given one of them up, he would certainly have been replaced by a Catholic.

So he traveled back and forth to serve both parishes until it became illegal to preach from the gospel. Sanders continued to preach to his rural congregation until he was forcibly prevented from doing so. Since he couldn't work there, he traveled back to London.

As he entered the city on Saturday, October 14, Sanders was met by Sir John Mordant, an advisor to Queen Mary, who warned him against preaching the next day. Sanders ignored his advice and gave his morning sermon, then, as he was preparing for the afternoon one, he was taken from his church and brought before the bishop, Sir John Mordant, and some chaplains. The bishop asked Sanders to write out his beliefs concerning transubstantiation and sent him to see the lord chancellor, who put him in prison.

After being imprisoned for fifteen months, during which he stayed loyal to his conscience, Sanders was brought to trial before the lord chancellor on charges of treason, heresy, and sedition. Presented with the paper he'd written earlier on transubstantiation, Sanders replied, "What I have written, I have written. I won't accuse myself of anything else. There's nothing you can bring against me."

After he was excommunicated and turned over to the legal authorities, the Bishop of London came to prison to strip Sanders of his offices on February 4. When he was done, Sanders told him, "I thank God I'm not of your church." On February 8, Sanders embraced the stake and kissed it, saying, "Welcome to the cross of Christ. Welcome everlasting life."

John Hooper

During the reign of King Edward, John Hooper served as bishop of two dioceses, always acting as Paul instructed bishops to act in his epistle to Timothy. He never looked for personal gain, only for the care and salvation of his flocks, giving away any money that came his way. Twice I [Foxe] saw Hooper's house filled with beggars and poor people who were eating at a table filled with meat, an event a servant told me took place every evening before Hooper sat down to eat his own dinner.

Hooper served as bishop for more than two years under Edward. When Edward died and Mary was crowned queen, Hooper was one of the first ordered to report to London and imprisoned. He remained there for eighteen months, gravely ill most of the time, forced to spend his own money to obtain food. On March 19, 1554, Hooper was called before the bishops of Winchester, London, Durham, Llandaff, and Chichester and deprived of his bishoprics. On January 22, 1555, The Bishop of Winchester called him in to demand he forsake his Protestant beliefs and accept the Pope as the head of the Church of England. If he did so, he would be pardoned — as many other English churchmen had been. Hooper refused.

On January 28, 1555, Hooper appeared before Winchester and others and was given another chance to accept the Catholic Church. This was the same day Rogers was appearing, and they met outside as they left the church with their guards.

"Brother Rogers," Hooper exclaimed, "should we take this matter in hand and begin to fry these fagots?"

"Yes, sir," Rogers replied, "by God's grace."

"Be sure, God will give strength."

Hooper was returned to Newgate Prison for six days on January 29; on February 4 the Bishop of London stripped him of all Church offices and Hooper was transported to Gloucester to be burned.

On February 5, Hooper was brought to the stake. He had been given packages of gunpowder by the guard, to hasten his death and lessen his suffering. These he put under his arms and between his legs. Three irons were brought to fasten him to the stake — one for his neck, one for his waist, one for his legs — but Hooper said they weren't necessary. Just the one around his waist was used.

After Hooper forgave the man who made the fire, it was lit, but the fire builder had used green wood, and even when it finally caught, the wind blew the flames away from Hooper. A second fire was lit, but it only burned low, not flaring up as it should have. When the fire was lit the third time, the gunpowder on Hooper went off, but even that didn't do much good because of the wind.

Even when Hooper's mouth was black and his tongue swollen, his lips continued to move until they shrank to the gums. He knocked on his breast with his hands until one of his arms fell off. Then he knocked with the other — fat, water, and blood dropping off the ends of his fingers — until his hand stuck to the iron around his waist.

Hooper was in the fire for over forty-five minutes, suffering patiently even when the lower part of his body burned off and his intestines spilled out. Now he reigns as a blessed martyr in the joys of heaven that are prepared for the faithful in Christ.

Rowland Taylor

The town of Hadleigh, in Suffolk, was one of the first towns in England to hear the Word of God from Thomas Bilney. Through his work, a great number of men and women in that parish became educated in the Scriptures, many of them having read the entire Bible. Some could have recited most of Paul's epistles by heart, and most were qualified to give a godly judgment in any matter of controversy. The town's children and servants were also brought up and trained in God's Word, so Hadleigh seemed more like a university town of educated people than a town of laborers. Even more importantly, those in the town were faithful followers of God's Word in their daily lives.

Hadleigh's pastor was Dr. Rowland Taylor, a doctor of both civil and Church law. At that time most pastors received a house and land to support themselves, but most rented the land out to farmers and appointed an uneducated priest to serve the town, living elsewhere and not really helping the people in their care. But Taylor lived in the town with his congregation, fulfilling Jesus' charge to Peter: "Peter, lovest thou me? Feed my sheep." He took every opportunity to gather his people together and teach them the doctrine of salvation.

Taylor's whole life was a blessing to the town. He was a humble man, easily approachable by the poor who came to him for help. He never hesitated to correct the rich, either, as a good pastor should. He was always a gentle man, without rancor or ill-will, ready to do good to all men, forgiving his enemies, and never trying to do evil to anyone. Anyone who was poor, blind, lame, sick, or had many children to support found Taylor to be a faithful provider, much like a father. He saw that his parish contributed generously to the poor among them and made a generous contribution to the alms box himself every year.

Taylor served the town of Hadleigh all the days of Edward VI. But after Edward's death the Catholics openly ignored the reformations made under Henry VIII and Edward, overthrew the doctrine of the gospel, and persecuted everyone who refused to abandon the Reformation's gains and accept the Pope as the head of the Church of England.

Soon a lawyer named Foster — an unskilled court steward — conspired with John Clerk to return Catholicism to Hadleigh. They hired John Averth, a money-grubbing, immoral man, to come to Hadleigh and reinstitute the mass, hastily constructing an altar in the town's church that was torn down the next day. They rebuilt the altar, this time setting guards to protect it overnight. The next day Foster, Clerk, and Averth brought in all the necessary implements and garments for the mass, setting out armed guards to prevent anyone from interfering.

Hearing the church bells ringing, Dr. Taylor assumed he was needed at his office, but found the church doors tightly locked. Gaining entrance through the chancel door, he saw Averth celebrating the mass, surrounded by guards with drawn swords.

"You devil!" Taylor shouted. "How do you dare enter this church of Christ and profane and defile it with this abominable idolatry?"

Foster stood up. "You traitor! Why are you disturbing the queen's proceedings?"

"I'm no traitor," Taylor called back. "I'm the shepherd of this flock, with every right to be here. I order you — you popish wolf — in the name of God, leave! Don't poison Christ's flock with your idolatry."

"Are you going to make a commotion and violently resist the queen's proceedings?" Foster demanded.

"I'm not making a commotion. You papists do that. I only resist your idolatries, which are against God's Word and the queen's honor, and subvert the country. Furthermore, you're breaking the law that says no mass may be said at an unconsecrated altar."

When Averth heard that, he began to move away from the altar. John Clerk commanded him to continue the mass while Foster's guards forcibly led Taylor out of his church.

Mrs. Taylor saw her husband being pushed out, fell to her knees, and said loudly, "I beg God, the righteous judge, to avenge the injury this popish idolater does to the blood of Christ!" They threw her out, too, and locked the doors against the people who were gathering outside.

A day or two later, Foster and Clerk complained about Taylor to Stephen Gardiner, Bishop of Winchester. When he was summoned to appear before the bishop, the townspeople begged Taylor to run away, knowing he was doomed if he went to London, but Taylor took his servant and obediently appeared before Winchester.

Winchester greeted Taylor in his usual manner, calling him a "knave, traitor, heretic" and other names.

"My lord," Taylor replied, "I am not a traitor or heretic, but a true subject and Christian. I came here at your command. Why did you send for me?"

"Are you come, villain? How do you dare look me in the face? Don't you know who I am?"

"Yes," answered Taylor, "I know who you are. You're Dr. Stephen Gardiner, Bishop of Winchester, lord chancellor — but still a mortal man. If I should fear your lordly looks, why don't you fear God? How can you look any Christian in the face? You have forsaken the truth, denied our Saviour Jesus Christ and His Word, and gone against your oaths. How will you look when you appear before the judgment seat of Christ and answer to the oaths you made to King Henry VIII and King Edward VI?"

"I did well in breaking those oaths and coming home again to our mother, the Catholic Church of Rome. I want you to do the same."

Taylor spent the next two years in prison, reading, preaching, and exhorting the great number of godly ministers that filled the country's prisons at that time, one of whom was Master Bradford. So many of them were locked up together that the jails began to resemble universities.

About the end of January 1555, Taylor, Bradford, and Sanders were called before the bishops of Winchester, Norwich, London, Salisbury, and Durham and charged with heresy. Given the opportunity to submit to the Pope and confess their errors, all three refused. On February 4, 1555, Edmund Bonner, Bishop of London, came to the prison to strip Taylor of his Church offices. Told to put on his vestments, Taylor refused.

"You won't?" Bonner sneered. "Then I'll *make* you!"

"You won't, by the grace of God."

Taylor was dressed by force so the ceremony could continue.

The next night, Taylor's wife and son were allowed to eat dinner with him, since the king's jailers tried to be as kind as possible, unlike the bishop's. His wife suspected that he would be taken away that night, so she watched the prison until he and his guards appeared at 2:00 A.M. The sheriffs allowed them a few minutes together to say good-bye, and Taylor encouraged them all to stay firm in their faith. That night he was taken to an inn named the Woolpack, where he stayed until the sheriff of Essex arrived at eleven the next morning. Taylor was put on a horse and led out of the inn's courtyard, where his servant, John Hull, and Taylor's son met them. Taylor was allowed to hold the boy, bless him, and say good-bye to his servant before being led off.

All the way, Taylor was joyful and happy, busily preaching to his guards and trying to convert them. In a few days, they arrived in Hadleigh, where Taylor was to be burned. The streets of the town were lined with townspeople crying and lamenting their pastor's fate, but Taylor's head was hooded until they reached the common, and he wasn't sure where he was until a guard told him.

"Thanks be to God!" he exclaimed. "I'm home!" He was taken off his horse and unhooded.

When the people saw his ancient face and long white beard, they began calling out encouragement, but Taylor had promised not to speak — probably under the threat of having his tongue cut out. After he gave away his clothing, he looked up and said two sentences: "Good people, I have taught you nothing but God's holy Word, and those lessons I took out of the Holy Bible. Today I come to seal it with my blood." He was promptly hit in the head by one of the guards.

After saying his prayers, Taylor stepped into the pitch barrel, folded his hands in prayer, and stood against the stake as the fire was lit. A man in the crowd hurled a piece of wood at him, hitting him in the head and bloodying his face. "Friend," Taylor said, "I have enough problems. Why was that necessary?" Then he recited the fifty-first psalm until Sir John Shelton hit him in the mouth. "Speak in Latin!" he demanded.

Taylor lifted up his hands. "Merciful Father of heaven, for Jesus Christ my Saviour's sake, receive my soul into Your hands." He stood still without moving or crying until Soyce struck him on the head with a halberd, spilling out his brains, and his corpse fell into the fire.

William Hunter

On March 26, 1555, William Hunter —a godly young man only nineteen years old — was martyred. His story should be an example to all Christian parents who find their emotions at odds with their convictions, for William's parents allowed their son to follow his beliefs, even though it led to his death.

William was apprenticed to a silk weaver in London. In the first year of Queen Mary's reign, his parish priest ordered him to receive communion at the Easter mass, which he refused to do. His master, afraid he himself would be in danger if William remained in his house, asked the boy to move back to his father's house in Brentwood for several weeks, which he did.

Five or six weeks later, William picked up a Bible he found in the chapel at Brentwood and began to read it aloud to himself. He was interrupted when Father Atwell came into the chapel. "Are you meddling with the Bible?" Atwell demanded.

"Do you know what you're reading? Can you expound the Scriptures?"

"I don't take it upon myself to expound the Scriptures," William explained. "I found it here and was reading it to comfort myself."

Father Atwell commented, "It hasn't been a happy world since the Bible was published in English."

"Oh, don't say that! It's God's book, from which we learn to know what pleases and displeases God."

"Didn't we know that before?"

"Not as well as we do now with the Bible available," William replied. "I pray we always have it with us."

Father Atwell fumed. "I know you! You're one of those who dislikes the queen's laws. That's why you left London. If you don't mend your ways, you and many other heretics will broil!"

"God give me grace to believe His Word and confess His name, no matter what happens," William retorted.

Atwell rushed out of the chapel, calling back, "I can't reason with you, but I'll find someone who can, you heretic!"

William stayed in the chapel and continued to read until Atwell returned with the vicar of Southwell. "Who gave you permission to read and expound on the Bible?" the vicar demanded.

"I don't expound on it, sir," William answered. "I only read it for comfort."

"Why do you need to read it at all?"

"I'll read it as long as I live. You shouldn't discourage people from doing so. You should encourage them."

"Oh, so you want to tell me what I should do?" the vicar muttered. "You're a heretic!"

"I'm not a heretic just because I speak the truth."

More words passed between them concerning the sacrament of communion, on which William explained his point of view. Accused of being a heretic, he replied, "I wish you and I were both tied to the stake, to prove which of us would defend his faith the longest. I think you'd recant first."

"We'll see about that!" the vicar replied, leaving to report the boy.

The vicar went directly to Master Brown, who called in William's father and the local policeman and demanded that Mr. Hunter go find his son, since William had wisely left town after his argument with the vicar. Mr. Hunter rode for two or three days to satisfy Brown, intending to go back and say he couldn't find the boy, when suddenly they met. Mr. Hunter told his son to hide; he would go back and say he couldn't find him.

"No, father," William said. "I'll go home with you so you don't get in trouble." As soon as they arrived in town, William was arrested and taken before Brown, who argued with him about transubstantiation. William was so firm in his beliefs that he enraged Brown, who sent him to Bishop Bonner in London.

William was put in the stocks at London for two days, fed only a crust of brown bread and a cup of water before he defended himself to the bishop. Getting nowhere with the boy, Bonner ordered him locked up in jail with as many chains as he could bear. "How old are you?" he asked William.

"Nineteen."

"Well, you'll be burned before you're twenty if you don't do better than you did today!"

William spent nine months in jail, appearing before the bishop six times, including the time he was condemned on February 9. That day the bishop made William his final offer:

"If you recant, I'll make you a freeman and give you forty pounds to set up a business. Or I'll make you the steward of my house. I like you. You're smart, and I'll take care of you if you recant."

William replied, "Thank you, but if you can't change my mind through Scripture, I can't turn from God for love of the world. I count all worldly things but loss and dung, compared to the love of Christ."

"If you die believing this way," the bishop continued, "you will be condemned forever."

"God judges righteously, justifying those whom man condemns unjustly," William maintained.

William was sent back to Newgate Prison for a month, then taken home to Brentwood for burning. When his parents visited him there, they encouraged him to remain faithful, saying they were proud to have a son willing to die for Christ's sake.

At the stake, William asked the people to pray for him. Master Brown sneered, "Pray for you? I wouldn't pray for you any more than I would for a dog!"

"I forgive you."

"I'm not asking for your forgiveness!" yelled Brown.

Seeing a priest approaching with a Bible, William called out, "Get away, you false prophet! Beware of them, people. Don't take part in their plagues."

The priest replied, "As you burn here, so you will burn in hell."

"You lie, you false prophet!" William cried. "Get out of here!"

A man in the crowd spoke up, "I pray God will have mercy on his soul."

"Amen, amen," answered the crowd.

As the fire was lit, William tossed his psalter to his brother.
"William," his brother called, "think of the holy passion of
Christ. Don't be afraid of death."

"I'm not." William lifted his hands to heaven and said,
"Lord, Lord, Lord, receive my spirit." Dropping his head into
the smoke, William Hunter gave up his life for the truth,
sealing it with his blood to the praise of God.

Rawlins White

Rawlins White fished for many years in the town of Cardiff, a man who was well-liked by his neighbors. During the
reign of King Henry VIII, he was a good Catholic, but when
Edward came into power, White became a great searcher of
the truth. He was a totally uneducated man, unable to read,
so he sent his young son to school, and when the boy had
learned to read, his father had him read the Bible and other
books to him every evening.

White enjoyed studying the Scripture so much that he soon
gave up his fishing to travel from place to place and instruct
others, taking his son everywhere with him. Although he never
learned to read, White did have a remarkable memory and
was able to cite from Scripture more accurately than many
educated men of the day. He soon became a well-known,
successful professor of the truth.

Five years after White began this work, Queen Mary took
the throne. White gave up preaching openly, but continued to
do so privately, bringing a great number of people to Christ.
As the persecutions increased, his friends urged him to sell his
goods, give the money to his wife and children, and go into
hiding, but White refused to deny Christ.

The town's officers soon captured White, taking him to the Bishop of Llandaff, who sent him to prison after having many arguments with him about theology. He was imprisoned in the castle of Cardiff for a whole year. Even though White knew he was doomed and his family would suffer terribly when he was gone, he continued to pray for and preach to the friends who regularly visited him this year.

At the end of this time, White was tried before the Bishop of Llandaff. The bishop made a long speech explaining why White was being tried, to which he replied, "My lord, I thank God I am a Christian, and I hold no opinions against the Word of God. If I do, I want to be corrected by the Word of God, as a Christian should be."

After discussing the charges back and forth for some time, the bishop suggested they take time to pray that God would change White's mind. "Ah, now you're doing the right thing!" White exclaimed. "If your request is godly and lawful, and you pray as you should, God will hear you. So go ahead. You pray to your God, and I'll pray to mine. I know my prayer will be answered."

When they were done, the bishop said, "How do you stand? Will you revoke your opinions or not?"

"Surely, my lord," White replied, "Rawlins you left me, and Rawlins you find me. By God's grace, Rawlins I will continue to be. Certainly, if your prayers had been just and lawful, God would have heard them, but you honor a false God and pray incorrectly, so God didn't answer your prayers. I'm only one poor, simple man, but God has heard my prayer and will strengthen me in His cause."

As the furious bishop was about to condemn White, someone suggested they have a mass, to see if that worked a miracle in the man. Rawlins White left to pray in private while they went about their mass, returning when he heard the elevation bell ring — the principle point in the mass's idolatry.

"Good people," he cried to the congregation, "bear witness on the day of judgment that I did not bow to this idol" [the host].

White was condemned and returned to prison in the Castle of Cardiff — a dark, horrible place. He was brought to his execution wearing his wedding shirt, an old russet coat, and an old pair of leather pants. On the way to the stake, he met his weeping wife and children, the sight of them making him cry, too, until he hit his chest with his hand and said, "Flesh, you're in my way! You want to live? Well, I tell you, do what you can, you won't win."

White went cheerfully to the stake, leaning against it for a while, then motioning to a friend in the crowd. "I feel my body fighting against my spirit and am afraid it will win. If you see me tempted, hold a finger up to me so I'll remember myself." As the smith chained him to the stake, White told him to tighten it well in case his body struggled with his soul.

They began to pile the straw and wood around White, who reached down and helped them pile it up the best he could. When a priest stood next to him to preach to the crowd, he listened respectfully until the man reached the sacrament of the altar, then called out, "Don't listen to this false prophet!"

The fire was lit. White held his hands in the flames until his sinews shrunk and the fat dropped away, only taking them out once to wipe his face with the fire. All the while he was suffering — which was longer than usual — he cried loudly, "O Lord, receive my soul. O Lord, receive my spirit!" until he could no longer open his mouth. At last the fire consumed his legs and his whole body fell over into the flames. Rawlins

White died for testifying of God's truth and was rewarded the crown of everlasting life.

George Marsh

George Marsh lived quietly for many years with his wife and children on a farm in the countryside. When his wife died, he attended the University of Cambridge to become a minister, serving for a while as Lawrence Sanders's curate. Marsh preached for some time before being arrested and imprisoned for four months by the Bishop of Chester, who did not allow him any visitors and had the names of any who asked for Marsh reported to him.

He was brought before Dr. Cotes several times but maintained the theology he had been taught during Edward's reign and would not be moved, although he did admit, "I want to live as much as you do. But I cannot deny my master, Christ, or He will deny me before His Father in heaven." Marsh was condemned as a heretic and turned over to the sheriffs.

Since he wasn't allowed any visitors in prison, Marsh's friends would stand by a hole in the outer prison wall and call out, asking how he was. He always replied that he was fine, anxious to die as a witness of God's truth and trusting Him to help him bear it bravely. On the day of his execution, Marsh was brought out in irons. Some people tried to hand him money, which criminals being executed would accept to bribe a priest to say masses for them, but Marsh told them to give their money to prisoners or the poor, not him.

Outside the city near Spittle-Boughton, by the stake, the deputy chamberlain of Chester showed Marsh the pardon he could receive from the queen if he recanted. Marsh said he would love to accept it, that he even loved the queen, but he could not recant.

The fire was poorly made, so Marsh suffered terribly, bearing it with patience. He had been in the fire for a long time — his flesh broiled and puffed up so much that the chain around him couldn't been seen — when he suddenly spread his arms and called, "Father of heaven, have mercy on me" and died. Many people who witnessed Marsh's death said he was a martyr who died with patience and godliness, which caused the bishop to preach a sermon saying that Marsh was a heretic, burned like a heretic, and was now a firebrand in hell.

William Flower

William Flower, sometimes called Branch, was born at Snow Hill, Cambridge. He entered the Abbey of Ely and was made a monk at the age of seventeen, observing all the rules of the order, becoming a priest, and celebrating mass. But at the age of twenty-one, Flower left the order, abandoned his habit, became a secular priest, and returned to Snow Hill. There he celebrated mass and taught children for about six months.

He moved to several other places before he settled in Tewkesbury for a while and married; then he moved to London. One Easter morning, Flower saw a priest giving communion to the people in St. Margaret's Church in Westminster. Suddenly offended at the ceremony and the priest, he drew his knife and slashed the priest on the head, arm, and hand, causing the chalice with its consecrated host to fall to the floor, where it mingled with the priest's blood.

When he was brought before Bishop Bonner, Flower admitted he had acted in an unchristian manner by striking the priest and should be punished for that. But as far as his beliefs about communion went, he refused to submit. He told the bishop that he could do as he chose with his body, but he had no power over his soul, which belonged to God.

Given a few hours to think about it, Flower returned to the bishop, who asked him to reconsider his views of communion. "I'll stand by what I've said," Flower stated. "Let the law punish me." Every time he was seen by the bishop, his answer was the same: "I have nothing to say. I've already said all I have to say, and I won't change that."

On April 24 Flower was brought to St. Margaret's churchyard to be burned. First his left hand was held behind him while his right hand was cut off, then the fire was lit. As he burned, he cried aloud three times, "O Son of God, have mercy upon me!" Then he spoke no more, holding the stump of his arm up as long as he could with his other hand.

John Cardmaker & John Warne

John Cardmaker was an observant friar before the dissolution of the abbeys. After that, he served as a married minister, then was appointed a reader at St. Paul's under Edward's reign. The papists in that church were so upset by Cardmaker's doctrine that they cut and mangled his gown with their knives.

At the beginning of Queen Mary's reign, Cardmaker was brought to London and jailed with Barlow, the Bishop of Bath. After the chancellor examined both men, he declared them faithful Catholics — probably so he could use them as an example to encourage others to recant, although they might have weakened, too. It is known that in every examination that followed, the chancellor held Barlow and Cardmaker up as examples of discrete, educated men. Whatever really happened, Barlow was freed and continued to bear witness to the truth of Christ's gospel during the rest of his life. Cardmaker was returned to jail while the Bishop of London announced to the public that he would shortly be freed after accepting transubstantiation and some other articles of faith. However, he was never set free.

John Warne, an upholsterer, was charged with not believing in transubstantiation and refusing to accept communion, charges he willingly pleaded guilty to. No matter what the bishop said or threatened, Warne refused to budge from his beliefs.

On May 30, John Cardmaker and John Warne were led to the stake together. Warne said his prayers, was bound to the stake, and the wood and reeds were piled around him; all that was needed was the torch. Meanwhile, the sheriffs had taken Cardmaker aside and were talking to him privately, until the crowd became convinced that he was about to recant. Cardmaker left the sheriffs, approached the stake, and knelt down to pray, still in his clothes. By now the people were sure he would be freed. When he finished his prayers, Cardmaker took off his clothing and kissed the stake, comforting Warne as they bound him, too.

Realizing that Cardmaker had refused to save himself, the crowd called out blessings to him as the fire was lit under both men.

Thomas Hawkes

On February 8, 1555, six men were brought before Bishop Bonner: Stephen Knight, William Pigot, Thomas Tomkins,

John Lawrence, William Hunter, and Thomas Hawkes. All of
them were condemned the following day.

Thomas Hawkes, a tall, good-looking man with excellent
qualities, was born in Essex and raised as a gentleman. He was
known for his gentle behavior toward others and his dedica-
tion to true religion and godliness. Hawkes entered into the
service of the Lord of Oxford, staying there as long as Edward
VI lived, enjoying a good reputation and being well-loved by
everyone in the household. But when Edward died, everything
suffered: religion decayed, the godly fell into danger, and the
houses of good men came on hard times. Rather than change
his religious beliefs to fit those of Queen Mary's court and the
Lord of Oxford's house, Hawkes left the nobleman's service
and returned home, hoping to worship in peace there.

Soon after, Hawkes had a son. Since he refused to have the
baby baptized in the Catholic Church, he put the sacrament
off for three weeks and was reported to the Earl of Oxford for
contempt of the sacraments. The earl was either unable or
unwilling to argue matters of religion with Hawkes; he sent
him to Bishop Bonner of London.

Hawkes told Bonner that he had nothing against baptism
itself, just against its Catholic embellishments.

"Would you agree to have your child christened by the
book that was set out by King Edward?" the bishop asked.

"Yes. That's exactly what I want," Hawkes replied.

When Bonner could not convince Hawkes that the
Catholic service was as effective as the Protestant one, he
called in Mr. Harpsfield, the archdeacon of London.

"Christ used ceremonies," Harpsfield began. "Didn't He
take clay from the ground, spit on it, and make the blind man
see?"

"I know that," Hawkes replied. "But He never used it in baptism. If you want to use it, use it as Christ did."

"Suppose your child should die unchristened?"

"So?"

"Why, then both you and your child would be damned."

"Don't judge further than you may by the Scriptures," Hawkes retorted.

"Don't you know your child is born in original sin?"

"Yes, I do."

"How is original sin washed away?"

"By true faith and belief in Christ Jesus," Hawkes replied.

"How can your baby believe?"

"His deliverance from sin is grounded in the faith of his parents."

"How can you prove that?"

"Saint Paul, in First Corinthians seven, verse fourteen, says: 'For the unbelieving husband is sanctified by the wife, and the unbelieving wife is sanctified by the husband; else were your children unclean; but now are they holy.' "

"Recant, recant! Don't you know that Christ said, 'Except ye be baptized, ye cannot be saved'?"

"Does Christianity depend on outward ceremonies?" Hawkes asked.

"Partly, yes. What do you think about the mass?"

Hawkes replied, "I say it's detestable, abominable, and useful for nothing!"

"Useful for nothing? What about the epistle and gospel?"

"That's good, if it's used as Christ left it to be used."

"How about the confessional?"

"That's abominable and detestable. It's blasphemy to call upon, trust, or pray to anyone but Christ Jesus."

"We don't ask you to trust anyone, just call on them and pray to them. You know that you can't speak with a king or queen without first speaking to someone else."

"You mean I should call on those I don't trust? Saint Paul said, 'How shall they call on him in whom they have not believed?'"

"Don't you want someone to pray for you when you're dead?"

"No," Hawkes replied. "Once you're dead, no man's prayers can help you. Unless you can prove otherwise by Scripture."

"Don't the prayers of the righteous prevail?"

"Only for the living. David said, 'None of them can by any means redeem his brother, nor give to God a ransom for them.'"

"What books do you have?"

"The New Testament, Solomon's books, and the Psalter."

"Will you read other books?"

"Certainly. If you give me the ones I want."

"What do you want?"

"Latimer's books, my lord of Canterbury's books, Bradford's sermons, and Ridley's books."

"Take him away! The books he wants all support his heresies."

The next day Fecknam came to talk to Hawkes. "Are you the one who won't have his child christened unless it's done in English and will have no ceremonies?"

"Whatever Scripture commands done, I will do," Hawkes replied.

They continued for a while, Hawkes standing his ground and quoting Scripture to prove each point they debated. The following day Dr. Chedsay and Bishop Bonner talked with Hawkes, asking him what he thought of the Catholic Church.

"It's a church of vicious cardinals, priests, monks, and friars, which I will never give credit or believe," he replied.

Bonner explained to Chedsay, "He won't come to my chapel or hear mass. His services have to be in English."

"Christ never spoke English," Chedsay replied.

"Neither did He speak Latin," Hawkes retorted. "What good does it do me to hear a language I don't understand?" Hawkes went on to say that the Catholic Church engaged in the worship of idols, praying to saints, holy bread, and holy wine, none of which are found in or commanded by Scripture. On February 9, 1555, he was condemned as a heretic. He remained in prison until June 10.

A little before his death, some of Hawkes's friends asked him a favor. They were afraid for their own lives and wondered how long faith could stand in the midst of the fire. Hawkes agreed to lift his hand over his head if the pain was tolerable and his mind was still at peace. When he had been in the fire so long that he could no longer speak, his skin had shrunk, his fingers had been burned off, and everyone thought he was dead, Hawkes suddenly raised his burning hands over his head and clapped them together three times! The people there — especially those who understood his gesture — broke into shouts of praise and applause as Thomas Hawkes sunk down into the fire and gave up his spirit.

7

Thomas Watts

Thomas Watts, of Billericay, Essex, was a linen draper. Knowing he would soon be arrested, he sold all the cloth in his shop, gave almost everything he owned to his wife and children, donated the rest to the poor, and waited. On April 26, 1555, Watts was arrested and brought before Lord Rich and others in Chelmsford on charges of not going to mass.

Anthony Brown, the judge, asked Watts where he'd learned his religion, to which he replied, "From you, sir. In King Edward's day you spoke against this religion. No preacher could say more than you did then. You said the mass was abominable and exhorted us not to believe them, saying we should only believe Christ. You said that anyone bringing a foreign religion in here was a traitor."

Brown turned to Lord Rich. "He's slandering me, my lord! What kind of criminal is he? If he talks like this to my face, imagine what he says to my back!"

Finally growing weary of Watts, the commissioners sent him to the Bishop of London, who brought the following charges against him.

- *Thomas Watts lived in Billericay, within the jurisdiction of the Bishop of London.*

Watts replied that this was true.

- *He did not believe in the sacraments or take part in them.*

Watts replied that he believed in all the sacraments according to Christ's institution, but not according to the Catholic Church. Once he had believed as a Catholic, but the Church deceived the people.

- *He believed — and taught others — that communion was only a remembrance of Christ's body and blood, nothing else.*

Watts said he believed Christ's body was in heaven, nowhere else. He would never believe His body is in the host.

- *He believed that the true presence of Christ's body and blood was not in the host but in heaven.*

Watts agreed that that was exactly what he believed.

- *He believed that the mass is full of idolatry, abomination, and wickedness, that Christ did not institute it, ordain it, or believe it was good.*

Watts said he still believed that and would never change his mind.

- *He believed confession to a priest was unnecessary and that all a man needed to do was believe and confess to God.*

Watts replied that no priest could absolve him of his sins, but he said it was a good thing to ask a priest for advice.

- *He believed that Luther, Wycliffe, Barnes, and all others put to death for their beliefs about communion were good men, faithful servants, and martyrs of Christ.*

Watts said that he didn't know the theology of the men they'd listed, but if they didn't believe the body and blood of Christ were physically in the sacrament, they were good Christian men.

- *He believed fasting, praying, and giving alms were useless. If a man was saved, he didn't need to do them; if he wasn't, doing them wouldn't save him.*

Watts denied he'd said that, saying he believed fasting, prayers, and giving alms were works of a lively faith.

- *He openly admitted that he refused to go to church and receive communion because that service was abominable. He also said other erroneous and arrogant things, serving as a bad example to the people present.*

Watts replied that was true, and he would die believing the same.

- *He was an open heretic, to be cursed by the Church and turned over to the secular authorities for punishment.*

Watts said he would submit to the law, trusting God would bless him even if he was cursed by men.

- *He said the Church of Rome was the synagogue of Satan.*

Watts said he believed the Pope was a mortal enemy of Christ and His Church.

- *All of the above charges are common knowledge in the area of Billericay.*

Watts replied that everything he'd said before was true.

From May 10-17 Watts saw one churchman after another, none of whom could make him move an inch from what he'd maintained all along. He was turned over to the sheriffs of London and imprisoned in Newgate until May 22 or June 9 before being transferred to Chelmsford, where he had dinner with Hawkes and others who'd been brought down for burning. Given the opportunity to speak to his wife and six children, he encouraged them to be faithful to their beliefs, no matter what; two of his children promptly offered to go to the stake with their father.

Watts kissed the stake before he turned to Lord Rich and warned him, "My lord, beware! You act against your conscience in this, and unless you repent, the Lord will revenge it, for you are the cause of my death."

Proclamation Against Books

About this time a book was brought into England that warned Englishmen of the Spaniards and disclosed some secret plans for the Church's recovery of abbey lands that had previously been confiscated. The book was titled *A Warning for England.*

On June 13, 1555, the king and queen banned all books that disagreed with Catholicism, specifically naming all books by the following authors: Martin Luther, Oecolampadius, Zwingle, John Calvin, Pomerane, John Alasco, Bullinger, Bucer, Melancthon, Barnardinus, Ochinus, Erasmus, Sarcerius, Peter Martyr, Hugh Latimer, Robert Barnes (Friar Barnes), John Bale (Friar Bale), Justus, Jonas John Hooper, Miles Coverdale, William Tyndale, Thomas Cranmer, William Turner, Theodore Basil (Thomas Beacon), John Frith, Roy. In addition, the book of common prayer in English that was used during King Edward's reign was banned.

Anyone owning any of these books was ordered to turn them in within fifteen days, and all civil authorities were given permission to search homes and arrest anyone possessing them.

Books supporting the Catholic Church were acceptable, including the *Primer in English,* which taught children to pray to Mary and the saints, and *Our Lady's Psalter,* which substituted Mary's name for God's in the psalms.

The apostles taught us that we are fully complete in Christ and need no one's intercession for our sins. And if idolatry is making an idol to be worshiped as a God, isn't it idolatry to worship Mary? If God hadn't explained His will to us in plain words, telling us exactly what to believe, how to worship, and how to be saved, perhaps Catholicism's use of mediators for reconciliation might have made sense, but God's Word plainly tells us that salvation and justification only come through Christ. Not believing what He promised is infidelity; following any other belief is idolatry. Yet the Church of Rome refuses to accept what God has freely given and will not seek salvation through Christ but through its saints and superstitions.

John Bradford

John Bradford was born in Manchester and educated until he was able to earn a living in the secular world, which he did successfully for several years before giving up his business affairs to study the gospel. Bradford left his study of secular law in London to enroll as a divinity student at Cambridge, working so diligently that he was awarded his master of arts degree within a year.

Immediately after, he was given a fellowship at Pembroke Hall, where Martin Bucer encouraged him to become a preacher. Bradford believed he wasn't educated enough to preach, to which Bucer replied, "If you don't have fine white bread, give the poor people barley bread or whatever else the Lord has given you." Finally convinced to preach during King Edward's reign, Bradford accepted the degree of deacon from Bishop Ridley, was licensed to preach and given a position at St. Paul's.

For the next three years, Bradford preached the gospel faithfully. He sharply reproved sin, sweetly preached Christ crucified, pithily spoke against heresies and errors, and earnestly persuaded his people to live godly lives. When Queen Mary took the throne, Bradford continued his work.

On August 13, 1553, Mr. Bourne, the Bishop of Bath, gave a sermon at St. Paul's Cross in London supporting the return of Catholicism under Mary. His words so angered the congregation that they threatened to pull him out of the pulpit. The more Bishop Bonner and the mayor of London tried to calm the crowd, the angrier everyone became, until Bourne actually began to fear for his life and asked Bradford to speak to the people.

As soon as Bradford moved to the pulpit, the crowd shouted, "Bradford! Bradford! God save your life, Bradford!" Bradford calmed the crowd down, and soon they all left peacefully for their homes.

Even though the mayor and sheriffs were there to see Bourne safely home, he refused to leave the church until Bradford agreed to accompany him, so Bradford walked closely behind Bourne, protecting him from harm with his own body.

Three days later, Bradford was summoned by the council and charged with sedition — for saving Bourne's life! — and with illegal preaching — although he had been asked to speak.

He was imprisoned for nearly a year and a half, until his hearing before the lord chancellor in January, 1555. There he was offered a pardon if he would recant his Protestant beliefs and rejoin the Catholic Church, as many preachers had already done. On July 29, the offer was repeated. Bradford urged the council not to condemn the innocent. If they believed he was guilty, they should pass sentence on him; if not, they should set him free.

In reply, the chancellor told Bradford that his actions at St. Paul's Cross had been presumptuous and arrogant in that he took it upon himself to lead the people. He was also charged with writing seditious letters.

The following day Thomas Hussey and Dr. Seton visited Bradford in prison. Both men urged him to request time to discuss his religious beliefs with learned men, saying this would remove him from immediate danger and look good to the council. Bradford refused. "That would make the people think I doubt the doctrine I confess. I don't doubt it at all."

Brought back before the council, which asked him to rejoin the Catholic Church, Bradford replied, "Yesterday I said I would never consent to work for the Pope. I say the same today." He was condemned and returned to prison.

All the time Bradford spent in prison, he continued his work, preaching twice a day to the many people allowed to visit him and administering the sacrament. Preaching, reading, and praying occupied his whole life; he only ate one small meal a day, and even then he meditated as he ate. Bradford's keepers thought so highly of him that he was often allowed to leave the prison unescorted to visit sick parishioners on his word that he would return by a certain hour. He was so precise in obeying the terms that he usually arrived back well before his curfew.

Bradford was a tall, slender man with an auburn beard. He rarely slept more than four hours a night, preferring to spend his time in writing, preaching, or reading. Once or twice a week he would visit the common criminals in the prison and give them money to buy food or other comforts.

One of his friends once asked Bradford what he would do if he were freed. Bradford said he would marry and hide in England while he continued to preach and teach the people.

One day in July, 1555, the keeper's wife warned Bradford that he was to be burned the following day.

"Thank God," he replied. "I've looked forward to this for a long time. The Lord make me worthy."

Bradford was transferred to Newgate Prison about eleven or twelve that night, the authorities hoping no one would be up to see him then, but a crowd of people watched him as he passed, prayed for him, and told him good-bye.

His execution was announced for four o'clock the next morning. No one was sure why such an unusual hour was chosen, but if the authorities hoped the hour would discourage a crowd, they were disappointed. The people waited faithfully at Smithfield until Bradford was brought there at nine in the morning, led by an usually large number of armed guards. Bradford fell to the ground to say his prayers, then went cheerfully to the stake with John Leaf, a young man of twenty.

John Leaf

John Leaf, who was burned with Bradford, was born in Kirby Moreside, York, a candle-maker's apprentice living in the parish of Christ's Church, London.

Brought before Bishop Bonner, Lamb admitted he did not believe the bread and wine were Christ's actual body and blood, but were a remembrance of them. He also stated that Catholic confession wasn't necessary and that a priest had no power to absolve sins.

Leaf was returned to prison until June 10, when Bonner saw him again and tried — by persuasion, threats, and promises — to convince the young man to change his mind. Getting nowhere, the bishop asked Leaf if he was one of Rogers's scholars. Leaf replied he was, that he believed the doctrine of Rogers, Hooper, Cardmaker, and others who had recently been killed for their testimony, and he would die for the same doctrine. "My lord," he said, "you call my opinion heresy. It is the true light of the Word of God." Unable to move the boy, Bonner condemned him and sent him back to prison.

It's said that shortly after this, two letters were brought to Leaf: one containing a recantation, the other a confession. When the recantation was read to him, he refused to sign it. When the confession was read, he took a pin, pricked his hand, and sprinkled his blood on the paper to show the bishop he was ready to seal his beliefs with his blood.

Bradford and Leaf went to the stake together, Bradford lying on one side of it to pray and Leaf on the other. After they had prayed silently for an hour, one of the sheriffs said to Bradford, "Get up and end this. The press of the crowd is great." They both got up. Bradford kissed a piece of firewood, then the stake itself before addressing the crowd.

"England," he cried, "repent of your sins! Beware of idolatry. Beware of false antichrists. See they don't deceive you!" Then he forgave his persecutors and asked the crowd to pray for him. Turning his head to Leaf, Bradford told him, "Be at peace, brother. We will have a happy supper with the Lord tonight." Both men ended their lives without fear, hoping to obtain the prize for which they had long run.

James Trevisam

James Trevisam was deathly ill, helpless, and lame, so sick he was unable to leave his bed. One evening his servant, John Small, was reading the Bible to Trevisam, Mrs. Trevisam, two men, and a woman, when an official entered his house and carried everyone but Trevisam off to prison, where they stayed for two weeks. He would have had Trevisam carried off, too, if some neighbors hadn't stopped him, but he did make the poor man put up two bonds to assure he would appear when called.

A few days later the parson of the church, Mr. Farthing, talked with Trevisam. Seemingly satisfied with his answers, the parson left the house. Along the way, he met with a Mr. Toller, who accused Trevisam of denying the sacrament of the altar, so the parson returned to Trevisam and discovered that Toller was right. He reported his findings to the Bishop of London.

On Sunday, July 3, 1555, Trevisam died of natural causes. The parson refused to let Mrs. Trevisam bury her husband in a coffin or in the church cemetery, forcing her to carry the body on a table to Moorfields, where it was buried in a sheet. That night Trevisam's body was dug up, the sheet stolen, and his body thrown naked on the ground. When the owner of the field saw the body the next day, he reburied it, and two weeks later he was called to answer charges against him. No one knows what happened to the field's owner after that.

John Bland

John Bland was a teacher before becoming the vicar of a congregation in Rolvendon, Kent. Thrown into Canterbury prison for preaching the gospel during Queen Mary's reign, he was freed once or twice by his friends' petitions, yet as soon as he was freed, he always returned to his Protestant preaching. Arrested a third time, Bland refused to promise his friends that he wouldn't preach his beliefs again, and they were no longer able to help him.

On November 26, two of Bland's parishioners, Richard and Thomas Austen, approached him after the service. "Parson," Richard Austen said, "you took down the tabernacle where the rood hung and other things. The queen has ordered that they be put up again, and we think you should pay for that. You go against the queen's laws when you say these are abominations."

"Mr. Austen," Bland replied, "if that's what I said, I'll say it again."

Thomas Austen replied, "Tell us what's devilish in the mass, then!"

"I often preached it to you. You didn't believe me then, and you won't now."

"You pulled down the altar. Will you rebuild it?"

"No. Not unless I'm ordered to, because I was ordered to take it down," Bland insisted.

On December 28, the priest of Stodmarsh was invited to say mass by the Austens. He was well into matins when Bland arrived, and when he finished, he said to Bland, "Your neighbor asked me to say matins and mass. I trust you won't disobey the queen's laws?"

"No," Bland replied, "I won't disobey the queen's laws, God willing."

Pretending he couldn't hear Bland's reply, the priest asked the question twice more, until Bland raised his voice so the whole congregation could hear his answer. The priest then sat down while Bland stood in the chancel door to give his address to the congregation. Bland explained his beliefs about the bread and wine, how Christ instituted the sacrament and how it had been perverted by the Catholic Church. In a few minutes he was stopped by the church warden and constable and locked in a side chapel until the mass was over.

On February 23 or 24, Bland was locked in Canterbury castle for ten weeks before being allowed to post bail. On May 18, he appeared before the Archdeacon of Canterbury, who demanded to know what Bland preached on communion. Bland refused to answer, saying they were trying to gather material to use against him and English law said he did not have to speak against himself. He was called again on May 21, again refusing to state his beliefs and requesting a lawyer.

On June 28, Bland reported to the secular authorities as ordered. They said they had nothing against him and ordered him to reappear seven weeks later, but when the date came, Bland was before the Church authorities and missed his court date. He was locked in Maidstone prison for that until February 18 or 19. After he would not promise to reform and be a good Catholic, Bland was sent to Canterbury castle until March 2.

Bland continued to be tossed to and fro, from prison to prison, session to session, until on June 13 he was brought before Richard Thornton, the Bishop of Dover; Robert Collins, the commissary; and Nicholas Harpsfield, Archdeacon of Canterbury. Under these three men a great number of Protestants were cruelly treated and killed at Canterbury, John Bland being one of the first. With him that day the following men were also tried: John Frankesh, Nicholas Sheterden, Thomas Thacker, Humphry Middleton, and William Cocker.

Bland pleaded guilty to the following charges:

- He believed the physical body of Christ was in heaven, not in the bread and wine.
- He believed it was against God's Word to have the sacraments administered in Latin and no one should accept any sacrament he could not understand.

On June 25, Bland appeared before the authorities for the last time and refused to accept the Pope's authority. He was condemned as a heretic and turned over to the secular authorities for burning.

Christopher Waid

Christopher Waid was a linen weaver from Dartford, Kent, condemned by Maurice, the Bishop of Rochester. On the day of his execution in July, the stake, reeds, and wood for his fire were taken out to Brimth, a gravel pit outside the village of Dartford.

At ten that morning, Waid and Margery Polley, of Tunbridge, passed by the site on their way into Dartford with the sheriffs. Seeing the crowd that was gathering at Brimth, Margery called to Waid, "Rejoice, Waid! Look at the crowd gathering to celebrate your marriage today!"

In town, Margery was locked up until the sheriff was done with Waid. Waid took off his clothes at an inn and put on a long white shirt brought by his wife. Then he was tied up and taken out to Brinth. Going right to the stake, he embraced it, set his back to it, and stepped into the pitch barrel. He was fastened to the stake by the smith with a hoop of iron.

As soon as he was set, Waid loudly recited the last verse of Psalms 86: "Show me a token for good; that they which hate me may see it and be ashamed; because thou, Lord, has helped me and comforted me."

Near the stake was a little hill with a makeshift pulpit on it. As Waid was praying, a friar entered the pulpit with a book in his hand, but Waid warned the people not to listen to the doctrine of the Catholic Church. He urged them to embrace the religion of King Edward's days, instead. While Waid spoke, the friar stood still in his pulpit; when Waid was done, he left without saying a word.

As the reeds were placed around him, Waid pulled them close, leaving an opening around his face so he could speak. The fire was lit, and Waid could be heard to say, "Lord Jesus, receive my soul!" Even when he was no longer able to speak, Waid continued to hold his hands up over his head toward heaven.

Carver & Launder

On July 22, 1555, Dirick Carver was burned at Lewes, Sussex; the following day John Launder suffered at Stening. These two men were arrested about the end of October, 1554, along with other men who were praying at Carver's house. After examination they were sent to Newgate Prison to wait for a hearing before Bonner, the Bishop of London, which occurred on June 8, 1555.

There they were examined on many point of religion, writing and signing their own confessions of faith. After the bishop spoke with them for some time, trying to convince them to recant and accept the Catholic Church, they were dismissed and returned to Newgate until June 10.

Dirick Carver confessed to the following points:

- He did not believe Christ's physical body was present in the sacrament.
- He did not believe there was any sacrifice in the mass and no salvation in a mass said in Latin.
- He believed in seeing a good priest for advice, but not for confession, which did nothing to save a man.
- He did not believe the Catholic doctrine agreed with God's Word. He believed that Bishop Hooper, Cardmaker, Rogers, and others recently burned were good Christians, martyrs who preached the true doctrine of Christ.

Since the queen's coronation, he had kept his Bible and psalter in English and read them. He had also had English prayers and services said in his home. Thomas Iveson, John Launder, and William Vesie, his fellow prisoners in Newgate, were arrested with him while hearing the gospel read in English.

John Launder confessed to the following:

- He was present in Carver's house with twelve others to hear the English service and prayers, being in town on business and hearing of the service.

- He believed that all the services, sacrifices, and ceremonies of the Catholic Church are full of errors, worth nothing, and against God's Word.
- He believed that the bread and wine were only a remembrance of Christ, not His actual body and blood.
- He believed the mass was directly against God's Word and Church.
- He believed confession to a priest was useless and no man can absolve another from his sins. A sinful man who regrets his sins before God and sins no more is forgiven.

On June 10, 1555, Carver, Launder, and others were brought before the bishop again. Carver was asked if he would recant or stand by his confession. "Your doctrine," he replied, "is poison and sorcery. If Christ were here you would put Him to a worse death than He was put to before. You say that you can make a god. You can make a pudding, too. Your ceremonies in the church are beggary and poison, and confession is contrary to God's Word. It's poison."

John Launder also remained firm in his confession, and both men were condemned.

When Dirick was brought to the stake, his book was thrown into the pitch barrel to burn with him, but he reached down, picked it up, and tossed it into the crowd. The sheriff ordered the book returned on pain of death, but Dirick immediately began to speak to the crowd.

"Dear brothers and sisters, I am here to seal Christ's gospel with my blood because I know it is true. You know the gospel — it's been preached to you here and all over England, even though it's not preached now. Because I will not deny God's gospel to obey man's laws, I am condemned to die. Dear brothers and sisters, if you believe in the Father, the Son, and the Holy Ghost, do the works of your belief and you will have everlasting life. If you believe in the Pope and his laws, you are condemned. Unless God has mercy on you, you will burn in hell forever."

The sheriff scoffed, "If you don't believe in the Pope, you are damned, body and soul! Speak to your God. Ask Him to deliver you now or strike me down as an example!"

"The Lord forgive you for your words," Dirick replied. "Dear brethren, if I have offended anyone by word or deed, I ask you to forgive me. And I forgive all you who have offended me in thought, word, or deed.

"O Lord, my God, You have written, 'He that loveth father and mother more than me is not worthy of me; and he that loveth son or daughter more than me is not worthy of me. And he that taketh not his cross and followeth after me is not worthy of me' (Matthew 10:37, 38). But You know I have forsaken all to come to You. Lord, have mercy upon me, for unto You do I commend my spirit, and my soul rejoices in You."

Thomas Iveson

Thomas Iveson was burned at Chichester the same month, having been arrested and tried with Carver and Launder.

When he was being urged to recant by Bishop Bonner, Iveson said, "I would not recant my beliefs for all the goods of London. I appeal to God's mercy and will have none of your church or submit to it. What I've said before I will say again.

Even if an angel came from heaven to teach me another doctrine, I would not believe him."

Iveson was condemned and burned, maintaining his faith until the end.

James Abbeys

One of the many who labored to keep his conscience clear in those troublesome times was James Abbeys, a young man forced to wander from place to place to avoid being arrested for practicing his faith. But when the time came that the Lord had another type of service for him, Abbeys was captured and brought before Dr. Hopton, the Bishop of Norwich.

The bishop examined Abbeys on his religion, using both threats and promises, until Abbeys finally yielded to the persuasion. When he was dismissed and about to leave the bishop, Abbeys was called back and given a sum of money, but once he left, his conscience bothered him terribly, since he knew he'd displeased the Lord by his actions.

Abbeys immediately returned to the bishop, threw the money at him, and said he was sorry he'd recanted and accepted the gift. The bishop and his chaplains went back to work, but this time Abbeys stood firm and was burned to ashes on August 2, 1555.

John Denley

In the midst of the persecutors destroying the flock of God there were many who were not clergymen but laymen supporting the persecution. One of them was Edmund Tyrel, a lawyer serving as justice of the peace in Essex.

One day as Tyrel was returning from the burning of some martyrs he met John Denley, a gentleman, and John Newman, both from Maidstone, Kent. The two men were traveling to visit some godly friends that day. Thinking they looked suspicious, Tyrel stopped them, searched them, and found written confessions of faith on both. He sent them to the queen's commissioners, who sent them to Bishop Bonner. On June 28, Denley made the following answers to the charges against him:

- *He was of the diocese of London.*

Denley said that was true.

- *He did not believe there was a catholic Church of Christ on earth.*

Denley replied that was not true. He believed there was a Church built on the prophets and apostles, with Christ as its head. This Church preaches God's Word truly and ministers the sacraments of baptism and communion according to the Word.

- *He did not believe the Church of England was part of the catholic Church.*

The Church of England presently is not part of the Church. It is now the church of the antichrist because it changed the testament of God and set up its own testament of blasphemy and lies.

- *He believed the mass was full of idolatry, evil, and against God's Word.*

As it stood now, Denley said, the mass was idolatry where the bread and wine themselves were worshiped. Christ's body is in heaven, not in the sacramental bread and wine, so we should not worship them.

● *He believed confession was contrary to God's Word.*

Denley said the Church had the power to punish him for his sins, but not to forgive him. Only God could do that.

● *He did not believe a priest could absolve him of his sins.*

He agreed to that charge.

● *He did not believe in the present forms of baptism, confirmation, orders, matins, evensong, the anointment or absolution of sick people, or making bread and wine holy.*

Denley replied that the Church had changed the sacrament of baptism and other sacraments by adding to them.

● *He believed there were only two Church sacraments — baptism and the Lord's Supper.*

Denley agreed to this.

● *He believed that Christ was in heaven, not in the bread and wine, and he refused to accept communion at the mass.*

Denley said that was also true.

Only July 5, Denley was condemned and turned over to the sheriffs. On August 8, he went to the stake cheerfully singing a psalm as the flames rose around him. One of his tormenters threw a piece of wood at him, hitting him in the face. "Truly," Denley said, "you have spoiled a good old song." He spread his arms again and continued singing until he died.

Around August 28, Patrick Packingham died in Uxbridge. He had been charged with refusing to remove his hat during mass. When Bonner urged him to recant, Packingham told the bishop that the Catholic Church was the church of Satan and he would never return to it.

John Newman was burned August 31 at Saffron Walden, and Richard Hook gave his life about the same time in Chichester.

Warne, Tankervil & Others

After this came the persecution of ten other true servants and saints of the Lord. Not saints that the Pope made or those mentioned in *The Legend of the Saints* or in *The Lives of the Fathers,* but those spoken of in Revelation: "These be they that follow the Lamb withersoever he goeth, and who have washed their robes and made them white in the blood of the Lamb." In a way, the Pope did make these people saints, for if he had not killed them, they would not be martyrs.

The ten were: Elizabeth Warne, George Tankervil, Robert Smith, Stephen Harwood, Thomas Fust, William Hall, Thomas Leyes, George King, John Wade, and Joan Lashford.

Now that the prisons of London were full and more prisoners were still arriving, the council and commissioners sent these ten people to Bonner at once, to make room for others.

Elizabeth Warne was the wife of John Warne, who had been burned earlier as a heretic. She was captured with others on January 1 in a house in Bow Churchyard, London, as they gathered for prayers, then was imprisoned until June 11 before being transferred to Newgate, where she stayed until July 2. On July 6, Elizabeth appeared before Bishop Bonner, along with the nine others listed above.

The chief charge against them all was not believing that the physical body and blood of Christ were present in the bread and wine, although there were other charges, such as not going to church, speaking against the mass, and hating the Catholic ceremonies and sacraments.

After being brought before Bonner several times, Elizabeth Warne told him, "Do whatever you want. If Christ was in error, then so am I." On July 12 she was condemned as a heretic and burned at Stratford-le-Bow in August.

George Tankervil, born in the city of York, lived in London. He was a Catholic in King Edward's days, but when the persecutions began under Queen Mary, Tankervil was disgusted by them and began to doubt the church. He asked God to show him the truth about transubstantiation — something he'd always had doubts about — and came to believe as the Protestants did on the subject. Moved to read the New Testament for himself, Tankervil soon turned from the Catholic Church entirely and began to try to convert his friends, work that soon brought him before the Bishop of London, who condemned him.

Tankervil was brought to St. Albans to die on August 26 and was locked in an inn there while the sheriffs attended a local wedding. Since he was forbidden communion, he asked for and received a pint of Malmsey and a loaf of bread, knelt down to make his confession to God, and read the institution of the Last Supper from the gospel. "Lord," he prayed, "You know I don't do this to usurp anyone's authority or in contempt of Your ministers, but only because I cannot have it administered according to Your Word." When he had finished, he received the bread and wine with thanksgiving.

Then Tankervil asked his host to build him a good fire. He took off his shoes and stockings and stretched his leg into the flame, pulling it back when the flames hit it, showing how his flesh wanted one thing and his spirit another.

About two o'clock the sheriffs returned to take Tankervil to Romeland, a green near the west end of the abbey church. A priest approached while the wood was being arranged around him, and Tankervil called out, "I defy the whore of Babylon! Fie on that abominable idol! Good people, do not believe him!" Embracing the fire, he bathed himself in it and, calling on the name of the Lord Jesus, was quickly out of pain.

Robert Smith was brought to Newgate on November 5. He was a tall, slender man, active in many things, especially painting, which he found relaxing. Once he was converted by the preaching and reading of Mr. Turner and others, he was very fervent in his religion. When Queen Mary came to the throne, Smith was fired from his clerkship in Windsor College, arrested, and brought before Bishop Bonner. Smith saw Bonner four times, answering all his questions boldly, arguing theology without fear — perhaps even a little rashly — until Bonner realized he would get nowhere and condemned him on July 12.

While he was in prison, Smith had been used by God to comfort those suffering with him. At the stake on August 8, he determined to do the same, telling everyone present he was sure his body would rise again. "And," he added, "I'm sure God will show you some sign of that." By the time he was nearly half burned and black from the fire, everyone thought Smith was dead, but he suddenly rose upright, lifted the stumps of his arms, and clapped them together joyfully before sinking back into the flames.

Stephen Harwood and Thomas Fust died about the same time as Robert Smith and George Tankervil, being tried and condemned with them. One was burned at Stratford and the other at Ware. William Hale died at Barnet.

Of the ten people sent to Bonner at once, six were executed at various places. Three others — George King, Thomas Leyes, and John Wade — became so sick in prison that they were moved to houses in London, where they all died. Their bodies were thrown out into the fields and secretly buried at night by the faithful. The last of the ten was Joan Laysh or Layshford. She was reprieved for a while but eventually martyred, too.

8

The Glovers

John, Robert, and William Glover were brothers living in the diocese of Lichfield and Coventry. John, the eldest, was a gentleman, the heir to his father's estate in the town of Manchester. He had inherited a considerable amount of land and money but was made even richer in God's grace and virtues when he and his brothers received God's holy gospel, living it in their lives and professing it zealously.

John took his faith so seriously that whenever it was necessary for him to devote himself to business matters, he sincerely believed he had failed God and despaired of his salvation. He suffered from these inner doubts and depression for five years, taking no pleasure in food, sleep, or life itself until the Lord released him from his discomfort. Finally, John gave most of his land for the use of his brothers and sisters in Christ and turned the rest over to his servants and managers so he could pursue his studies of the gospel. This took place at the end of King Henry VIII's reign and continued during most of King Edward's.

When the persecution began under Queen Mary and the Bishop of Coventry heard of John's reputation, he ordered the mayor and officers of Coventry to arrest him. But God, seeing His old and trusty servant of so many years already suffering from his inner torments, would not have him suffer physically, and the mayor warned John, who fled the house and hid with his brother William. Unfortunately, Robert was seriously ill in bed and there wasn't time, or they were afraid to move him. When the searchers arrived at the house, Robert was the only brother found and taken to the sheriff.

The sheriff said that Robert had not been ordered arrested and did what he could to have him released, but was forced to imprison him against his will, at least until the bishop arrived in town to make a final decision.

In prison, Robert was visited by several of his friends who urged him to post a bond for his release. They even explained how he could flee the area without forfeiting his bond. But Robert refused. "If I make any attempt to pull my own neck out of the collar," he told his wife, "I will give offense to my weak brethren in Christ and advantage to those who slander God's Word. It will be said that I encouraged others to accept the perils of the world but was unwilling to do the same."

Robert remained in jail in Coventry for ten or eleven days with no warrant for his arrest and no charges being made against him, until the Bishop of Coventry arrived in town. They had a short disagreement over the mass, then the bishop decided to let the full examination wait until he'd finished his work in town. The next day Robert was transferred to Lichfield.

"Jephcot put me into a prison that night, where I stayed until I was condemned, in a narrow, strong building, very cold, with little light, and a bundle of straw instead of a bed." Robert, still very sick, was allowed to buy himself a bed, but nothing more. "I was allowed no help, day or night, nor any company, notwithstanding my great sickness — no paper, no pen or ink, no books except my Latin New Testament and a prayer book I had to buy for myself."

Two days later the chancellor visited Robert in his cell, urging him to rejoin the Catholic Church. "I refuse to be ruled by a church that is not governed by the Word of God," he replied. The chancellor decided not to argue religion at that time and left Robert alone for the next eight days, until the bishop returned.

At that time Robert was taken before the bishop, who asked him how he liked being in prison, then urged him to rejoin the Church. "Where was your Church before King Edward's time?" he sneered.

Robert replied that his Church was built on the foundation of the apostles and prophets, Christ being the cornerstone. "And this Church has been from the beginning, though it doesn't have a glorious show before the world, always being afflicted and persecuted."

The bishop examined Robert on the usual questions of confession and the sacraments, and Robert stood firm in his faith. He was speedily condemned and burned.

After his brother's death in his place, John Glover came to care even less for his own life, but his friends convinced him to stay in hiding, since his death could not save his brother. Although he suffered mentally and physically, John persevered until, at the end of Queen Mary's reign, a new search was made for him.

When the sheriff and his officers arrived at the house, John was alone in his room. Hearing the commotion, he quietly latched the door. One of the officers was about to force the door open, but he was called away by another who said the room had already been searched. The officers did find John's wife, Agnes, however. She was taken to the bishop, forced to recant, and eventually released, while John was forced to hide in the woods. Worry about his wife and exposure to the weather wore John down so much that he contracted a fever and soon died. He was buried by his friends in the churchyard without the services of a priest.

Six weeks later the chancellor, Dr. Dracot, sent for the church's pastor and demanded to know why a heretic was buried in his churchyard. The pastor replied that he'd been sick at the time and knew nothing about the burial. When Dracot demanded that John's body be dug up and thrown into the road, the parson complained that the body would smell so badly no one would do the job.

"Well," said Dracot, "take this letter and pronounce him a damned soul from the pulpit. A year from now, when his flesh is gone, take up his bones and throw them in the road, where carts and horses will tread on them. Then I'll come and consecrate the place where he lay in the churchyard."

Soon William died. When the people of Wem brought his body to the parish church, the curate rode to the bishop for advice on how he could prevent the burial. After the body had lain in the church for a full day, Richard Maurice, a tailor, decided to bury it himself during the night, but he was stopped by John Thorlyne and others.

A day later, the curate returned with the bishop's letter, which stated that William Glover was denied a Christian burial and must be taken away by his friends. By now his body had begun to decompose, and no one could bear to go near it, so he was dragged into a field by horses and buried there.

The same fate befell Edward Burton, a lawyer from Chester, who died the day before Queen Elizabeth was crowned. The local curate, John Marshall, refused to let him be buried in the churchyard, so Burton was interred in his own garden, no doubt as near the kingdom of heaven as if he'd been buried by the church.

William Wolsey & Robert Pygot

On October 9, 1555, William Wolsey and Robert Pygot of Wisbeach were condemned at Ely by John Fuller, the bishop's chancellor; Dr. Shaxton, his suffragan; Robert Stewart, the dean of Ely; and John Christopherson, the dean of Norwich.

William Wolsey was a policeman in the town of Wells who was accused by Richard Everard, a justice, and put in jail.

Before he was condemned, Dr. Fuller and others visited Wolsey and urged him to return to the Church, but got nowhere. Before he left the prison, Fuller gave Wolsey a book by Dr. Watson, the bishop of Lincoln, hoping that might show Wolsey where his theology was wrong and convince him to recant his current beliefs. As Wolsey suspected, he found the book full of opinions that were contrary to Scripture, so he returned it to the chancellor on his next visit.

That night when Dr. Fuller looked at his book, he found Wolsey had written notes in it — in ink. "This obstinate heretic has ruined my book!" he complained. Still, as the time approached for Wolsey to appear in court, Fuller went back to visit him again. "You bother my conscience," he admitted. "Leave, but watch what you say, so no one complains to me again. Come to church when you want to, and if someone complains about you, I'll sent them away."

"Doctor," Wolsey replied, "I was brought here by the law, and I will be freed by the law." Brought to trial, Wolsey was imprisoned in the castle at Wisbeach for some time.

About the same time, Robert Pygot, a painter, was accused of not going to church. Appearing before the judge at Wisbeach, he was asked why he had left the Church.

"Sir," he replied, "I am not out of the Church. I trust in God."

"But this isn't a church. This is a hall."

"True, but he that is in the true faith of Jesus Christ is always in the Church."

"Ah! You know too much for me to talk to. I'll send you to those with more learning."

Pygot joined Wolsey in jail until the court session was over and they were transferred to Ely. On October 9, 1555, they were both examined by Dr. Fuller on their beliefs, especially those on transubstantiation. After their sentence was read and a sermon preached, they were bound to the stake with a chain. Asked once more to recant his errors, Wolsey replied, "I ask God to witness that I am not wrong in any point of the Holy Bible. I hold it to be sound doctrine for my salvation and for others until the end of the world. Whatever my enemies say, I ask God to forgive them."

Just before the fire was lit, someone brought a pile of English New Testaments to be burned with them. "Oh!" said Wolsey, "give me one of them." Pygot asked for one, too, and they died together, singing Psalms 106 and clasping the testaments to their hearts.

Bishop Ridley

The same day that Wolsey and Pygot died in Ely — October 16, 1555 — two other outstanding leaders of the Church died at Oxford: Bishop Ridley of London and Bishop Hugh Latimer of Worcester.

Among those martyred for the true gospel of Christ in Queen Mary's time, Dr. Ridley serves as an excellent example of spiritual inspiration and godly education. Born in Northumberland, Ridley learned his grammar as a child in Newcastle and attended Cambridge, where he soon became well-known for his intelligence and advanced rapidly, becoming a doctor of divinity and the head of Pembroke Hall. After that, he traveled to Paris, was made Henry VIII's chaplain on his return, and appointed Bishop of Rochester by the king. In King Edward's days he served as the Bishop of London.

Ridley worked so diligently at preaching and teaching his flock the true doctrine of Christ that his parishioners loved him the way a child loves his father. People swarmed to his sermons like bees to honey, knowing their bishop not only preached Christ but lived a pure, holy life. He was well-educated, with a remarkable memory, and even his enemies admired his educated writing, pithy sermons, and lectures.

Besides all this, Ridley gave excellent advice, being very judicious in all his doings. He was merciful and careful when dealing with Catholics during Edward's reign, winning many of them over through his gentle teaching.

Ridley was an attractive man who never held a grudge and always forgave any injury done to him. He was kind and affectionate to his relatives but expected as much from them in their daily lives as he did from any other parishioner. Any family member doing evil could expect no special treatment from Ridley; those who lived honest, godly lives were his brothers and sisters, no matter who they were.

Ridley lived a well-regulated, strict life. As soon as he was dressed in the morning, he prayed on his knees for half an hour in his room. Then he would go to his study, where he worked until the ten o'clock prayers for his household. After prayers, he would go to dinner, where he talked very little, then return to his study until afternoon prayers at five. He would have his dinner, go back to his study until eleven, then retire for the night.

At his manor in Fulham, he would give a lecture to his family every day, beginning at Acts and going through all Paul's epistles. He gave every member of his household who could read a copy of the New Testament. He was extremely careful to see that his family served as good examples of virtue and honesty. In short, he was so godly and virtuous himself that those qualities reigned in his whole household.

When Bishop Ridley was at home in Fulham, he always had his next-door neighbor, Mrs. Bonner, and her sister over for supper and dinner, giving her the honored seat at the end of the table, even if someone else of importance was present. "By your lordship's favor," he would tell his guest, "this place is for my mother Bonner." Mrs. Bonner was the mother of the man who would later become Bishop Bonner during Queen Mary's time — the man responsible for the deaths of many Protestants, including Ridley.

Dr. Ridley was first brought to the gospel through Bertram's *Book of the Sacrament* and discussions with Bishop Cranmer and Peter Martyr. When Queen Mary came to the throne, he was arrested. First imprisoned in the Tower of London, he was then sent to jail in Oxford with the Archbishop of Canterbury and Hugh Latimer. After being condemned, he was kept in the house of Mayor Irish from 1554 until his death in 1555.

Bishop Latimer

Bishop Latimer was the son of Hugh Latimer of Thurcaston, Leicester, a farmer with a good reputation. At the age of four, he was sent to school and trained in literature; at fourteen, he entered the University of Cambridge to study divinity, becoming a scrupulously observant Catholic priest. At first Latimer was a bitter enemy of the Protestants, opposing the works of Philip Melancthon and Master Stafford. But Thomas Bilney felt pity for Latimer and decided to try to win him to the true knowledge of Christ. Bilney asked Latimer to hear his confession of faith, and Latimer was so moved by what he heard that he left his study of the Catholic doctors to learn true divinity. Where before he was an enemy of Christ, he now became a zealous seeker of Him, even asking Stafford's forgiveness before that man died.

In 1529 a great number of friars and doctors of divinity from all the schools at Cambridge began to preach against Latimer and his new beliefs. Dr. West, Bishop of Ely, forbade him to preach within the churches of that university, but Dr. Barnes, the prior of the Augustine friars, licensed Latimer to preach in his church. Like a true disciple, Latimer spent the next three years working to convert his brothers at the university and the parishioners of his church, speaking Latin to the educated and English to the common people.

Latimer and Bilney stayed at Cambridge for some time, having many conversations together; the place they walked soon became known as Heretics' Hill. Both of them set a good Christian example by visiting prisoners, helping the needy, and feeding the hungry.

After preaching and teaching in Cambridge for three years, Latimer was called before the cardinal for heresy. At this time he bent to the will of the Church and was allowed to return to the university, where he met Dr. Buts, Henry VIII's doctor and supporter. Latimer joined Buts in Henry's court for some time, preaching in London, but became tired of court life and accepted a position in West Kingston that was offered him by the king. There he diligently instructed his parish and everyone in the nearby countryside.

It didn't take Latimer long to infuriate a good number of country priests and higher Church doctors with his beliefs on reform. Latimer was called before William Warham, Archbishop of Canterbury, and John Stokesley, Bishop of London, on January 29, 1531. He was kept in London for some time, being called for examination three times a week, until he wrote to the archbishop and said he was too ill to see him anymore. In the same letter, Latimer complained that he was being kept from his parish without just cause, for preaching the truth about certain abuses within the Church. Eventually Latimer seems to have accepted the charges against him (although there is no proof of this), and he was freed through the efforts of Buts, Cromwell, and the king.

In time, Henry VIII made Latimer the Bishop of Worcester, where he served faithfully, although the dangerous times prevented him from doing everything he wanted to. He wasn't able to rid his diocese of its superstitions, but did what he could within the Catholic Church, helping his parishioners exclude as much superstition as possible from their lives and worship. Even then, he continued to be harassed by other members of the clergy.

When the Six Articles were passed, Latimer voluntarily resigned his post, as did Shaxton, the Bishop of Salisbury.

Latimer went to London, where he was harassed by the bishops and imprisoned in the Tower until King Edward took the throne. On his release, Latimer went back to work, preaching twice every Sunday and once every weekday, unlike many clergymen who ignored their duties during Edward's reign. He was now sixty-seven years old and suffering from an injury received by the fall of a tree.

Not long after King Edward's death, Latimer was arrested on Queen Mary's command and thrown back into the Tower of London, where he suffered greatly. He was transferred to Oxford with Cranmer, the Archbishop of Canterbury, and Ridley, Bishop of London, to answer charges made by Gardiner, the Bishop of Winchester.

Because of his age, Latimer wrote less than Ridley and Cranmer while in prison, devoting himself more to prayer. He prayed about three main concerns:

- Since God had appointed him a preacher, Latimer asked Him for the grace to stand to His doctrine until his death.
- He asked God to restore His gospel to England once again.
- He prayed for the accession of Elizabeth, asking God to make her a comfort to the comfortless realm of England.

In time, all three of Latimer's prayers would be answered.

Ridley & Latimer

On September 30, 1555, Ridley and Latimer appeared together in Oxford before a panel of bishops to answer the charges of heresy that had been brought against them. Ridley was examined first.

The Bishop of Lincoln began by urging Ridley to recant and submit himself to the Pope. "If you will renounce your errors, recant your heretical and seditious opinions, consent to yield yourself to the undoubted faith and truth of the gospel ... authority is given to us to receive you, to reconcile you, and upon due penance to join you into Christ's Church." The bishop stressed three points:

- That the Pope was descended from Peter, who was the foundation of the Church.
- That the early Church fathers confessed the Pope's supremacy in their writings.
- That Ridley once believed this himself.

Ridley replied to the three points. First, he said, it was not Peter who was the Church's foundation, but Peter's confession that Christ was the Son of God. This belief is the foundation of the Church, not a mere man.

Secondly, the Bishop of Rome was supreme in the early Church because the city of Rome was supreme in the world of the day, not because he had any more religious power than other bishops. As long as the diocese of Rome was true to the gospel, its bishop deserved respect from everyone in the Church, but as soon as they began setting themselves above kings and emperors for their own honor, the bishops of Rome became anti-Christian.

To the last point, Ridley admitted he did once believe as they did, just as Paul was once a prosecutor of Christ.

The Bishop of Lincoln cut Ridley short, reminding him of the panel's power to either accept him back into the Church or excommunicate him. Anything they did would receive the support of the queen, who was a faithful member of the Church. The following article were then put forward against him (and Latimer):

- He maintained that the true body of Christ was not present in the bread and wine.
- He taught that the bread and wine remained bread and wine after consecration.
- He believed that the mass is not a propitiatory sacrifice for the living and the dead.
- That Dr. Weston and others declared these beliefs heretical.
- That all of the above is true and well-known.

Ridley was asked to reply to the charges with simple yes or no answers and was promised that he could amend his answers the next day, when he'd had more time to think about them. Before he answered, Ridley protested that whatever he said, he would be saying it unwillingly and his answering would not indicate that he accepted either the panel's or the Pope's authority over him.

To the first charge, he said that Christ's body and blood were present spiritually in the bread and wine, but not physically. To the second, he replied that the bread and wine remain bread and wine after consecration. To the third, he said that Christ made one perfect sacrifice for the sins of the whole world. Communion was an acceptable sacrifice of praise and thanksgiving, but saying it removed man's sins implied that Christ's work was not enough. To the fourth, Ridley replied that his beliefs had been declared heretical by Dr. Watson, but unjustly. To the fifth, that he believed exactly what he said, although he didn't know what everyone thought of his beliefs.

Ridley was dismissed until the following day and Latimer was brought in. As with Ridley, the bishop urged Latimer to give up his beliefs and rejoin the Catholic Church, which was again universally accepted. He was then asked to reply to the same charges as Ridley.

"I do not deny," he said in answer to the first charge, "that in the sacrament, by spirit and grace, is the very body and blood of Christ. Every man receiving the bread or wine spiritually receives the body and blood of Christ. But I deny that the body and blood of Christ is in the sacrament the way you say it is."

To the second, he replied, "There is a change in the bread and wine, and yet the bread is still bread and the wine is still wine."

On whether the mass is a sacrifice for sins, Latimer replied, "No. Christ made one perfect sacrifice. No one can offer Him up again. Neither can the priest offer Him for the sins of man, which He took away by offering Himself once for all upon the cross. There is no propitiation for our sins except the cross."

When Latimer was asked about his beliefs being called heresy, he replied, "Yes, I think they were condemned. But He that will judge us all knows they were condemned unjustly." Latimer was also dismissed until eight o'clock the next morning.

Ridley arrived on October 1 with his answers to the charges written out, asking permission to read them to the crowd that filled St. Mary's Church. But he was forced to turn his papers over to the bishops first, and they declared them heretical, refusing to read them aloud. In return, Ridley refused to answer their questions, saying all his answers were contained in his written replies. He was condemned as a heretic and turned over to the secular authorities for punishment.

Latimer was brought in. He agreed to answer the panel's charges again, but his answers were the same as the day before and he refused to recant. He was also condemned and turned over to the authorities.

The morning of October 15, the Bishop of Gloucester (Dr. Brooks) and the vice-chancellor of Oxford (Dr. Marshall), along with others from the university, arrived at Mayor Irish's house, where Ridley was being held a prisoner. Ridley was given the opportunity to rejoin the Church. When he refused, they forced him to go through the ceremony expelling him from the priesthood. The ceremony over, Ridley read a petition to the queen asking that she help Ridley's sister and brother-in-law and others who had depended on him for their support. Dr. Brooks promised to forward the petition to the queen, but doubted she would honor it.

That night Ridley's beard and legs were washed. At supper, he invited everyone in the mayor's house to his burning, as well as his sister and brother. When the mayor's wife began to cry, he comforted her by saying, "Quiet yourself. Though my breakfast will be somewhat sharp and painful, I'm sure my supper will be pleasant and sweet."

Ridley and Latimer were to be burned on the north side of Oxford, in a ditch by Baliol College, well guarded by the queen's orders. When everything was ready, they were brought out by the mayor and bailiffs. Ridley wore a furred black gown, velvet nightcap, and slippers. Latimer wore a worn frock, a buttoned cap, and a new long shroud hanging down to his feet.

Looking back, Ridley saw Latimer following him. "Oh. Are you here?" he called.

"Yes. As fast as I can follow," Latimer answered.

Ridley reached the stake first. Holding up his hands, he first looked toward heaven. When Latimer arrived, Ridley ran to him cheerfully, held him, and kissed him, saying, "Be of good cheer, brother, for God will either assuage the fury of the flame or else strengthen us to bear it." After they said their prayers, the two men talked quietly together for a little while, but no one knows what they said.

The officers prevented Ridley and Latimer from answering the sermon that was given by Dr. Smith. They would be allowed to speak only if it were to recant.

"Well, then," said Ridley, "I commit our cause to Almighty God, who shall impartially judge all."

Latimer added, "Well, there is nothing hid but it shall be made manifest."

Ridley cheerfully gave away his clothing and other items he possessed, then asked Lord Williams to do what he could to help those who depended on him for their living. The chain was fastened around the two men. "Good fellow, tie it tight, for the flesh will have its way," Ridley commented. Then his brother brought him a bad of gunpowder to hang around his neck. "I will take it to be sent by God, therefore I will receive it as sent of Him. And do you have some for my brother?" Told he did, Ridley sent his brother to Latimer before it was too late. Then they brought a torch and laid it at Ridley's feet.

"Be of good comfort, brother Ridley, and play the man," Latimer called. "We shall this day light such a candle by God's grace in England, as I trust shall never be put out."

When Ridley saw the flames leap up, he cried with a loud voice, "Lord, into Thy hands I commend my spirit. Lord, receive my spirit!"

Latimer cried as vehemently on the other side, "O Father of heaven, receive my soul!" He received the flame as if embracing it. After he stroked his face with his hands and bathed them a little in the fire, Latimer died with little visible pain.

But Ridley suffered longer because the fire did not flare up on his side of the stake, and he called out to them, asking them to let the fire come to him. His brother-in-law, misunderstanding the problem, covered Ridley with even more wood, which made the fire burn stronger on the bottom but kept it from flaring up as it should have. It burned all Ridley's lower parts before ever touching his upper body, which made him leap up and down under the wood piled around him as he cried, "I cannot burn!" Even after his legs were consumed, his shirt was still untouched by the flames. He suffered in terrible pain until one of the onlookers pulled off the wood that was smothering the flames. When Ridley saw the fire flame up, he leaned toward it until the gunpowder exploded. He moved no more after that, falling down at Latimer's feet.

The sight of Ridley and Latimer's struggle moved hundreds in the crowd to tears, seeing years of study and knowledge, all the godly virtues, so much dignity and honor — all consumed in one moment. Well, they are gone, and the rewards of this world they already have. What a reward remains for them in heaven on the day of the Lord's glory, when He comes with His saints!

Ridley's Farewell

Dr. Ridley wrote the following letter to all his friends in Christ before his death:

As a man about to take a long journey naturally wants to say good-bye to his friends, so I, expecting to leave you any day now, want to bid all my sisters and brothers here on earth good-bye.

Farewell, my dear brother George Shipside, who has always been faithful, trustworthy, and loving. Now in the time of my cross, you have been my most friendly, steadfast supporter, always serving God's cause.

Farewell, my sister Alice [Shipside's wife]. I'm glad to hear that you have accepted Christ's cross, which is now lain on your back as well as mine. Thank God for giving you a godly, loving husband; honor and obey him, according to God's law. Honor your mother-in-law and love everyone in his family, doing them as much good as you can. As for your children, I have no doubt that your husband will treat them as though they were his own.

Farewell, my dearly beloved brother, John Ridley, and you, my gentle and loving sister, Elizabeth. The tender love you were said to have for me above the rest of your family binds me to you in love. I wish I could repay you with deeds instead of words. I say good-bye to your daughter Elizabeth, who I love for her meek, gentle spirit. This is a precious thing in the sight of God.

Farewell, my beloved sister of Unthank, with all your children, nephews, and nieces. Since the death of my brother Hugh, I wanted to treat them as my own children, but the Lord God must and will be their Father, if they love and fear Him and live according to His law.

Farewell, my beloved cousins, Nicholas Ridley of Willimountswicke and your wife. I thank you for all the kindness you showed me and the rest of our families. Since God has made you a leader of our family and given you His gifts of grace above others, continue in truth, honesty, righteousness, and godliness and resist falsehood, unrighteousness, and ungodliness, which are condemned by the Word of God.

Farewell, my young cousin, Ralph Whitfield. Oh, your time was very short with me! I wanted to do good for you, but all you received was loss. I trust God will make that up to you.

Farewell, my family and countrymen; farewell in Christ to you all. The Lord knows I wanted to bring Christ's blessed gospel to your all; it was my duty as a minister.

I warn you all: Do not be ashamed by my death. I think it is the greatest honor of my life and thank God for calling me to give my life for His sake and in His cause. He gave the same honor to the holy prophets, His dearly beloved apostles, and His blessed chosen martyrs. I have no doubt that I am dying for God's cause and the cause of truth. Having a heart willing to stand for Christ to the death is an inestimable and honorable gift from God, given only to the true elect and dearly beloved children of God and inheritors of the kingdom of heaven. All of you that love me should rejoice that I, a sinful and vile wretch, was called to give up this temporal life in defense of His eternal, everlasting truth.

You, my family and countrymen, know you will always have reason to rejoice and thank God, and I know you will find favor and grace in my cause, for the Lord said He will be full of mercy to those who love Him.

Through the goodness and grace of Almighty God, the Church of England has recently enjoyed great substance, great riches of heavenly treasure, great plenty of God's true Word, the correct administration of Christ's holy sacraments — the whole profession of Christ's religion. It also observed the Lord's Supper correctly, observing Christ's commands. Thanks was given for the bread and wine, and the Lord's death was commemorated. The bread was broken in remembrance of Christ's body being torn upon the cross, the cup was shared in remembrance of Christ's shed blood, and everyone received both.

All this was done in English, so everyone would understand and give God the glory. Recently, all the services of this Church were performed in English according to the command of the Lord and Paul's doctrine, so people could understand and profit from them.

The Church of England also had holy, wholesome sermons urging people to lead godly lives, as well as those condemning the vices that used to reign in England. It had articles of belief grounded in Scripture that could have expelled the errors and heresies almost overgrowing the Church.

But alas, lately thieves have come in and stolen all this treasure. These robbers have robbed the Church of England of all its holy treasure, carried it away, and overthrown it. Instead of God's holy Word and true sacraments, they added their foolish fantasies and ungodly traditions.

Instead of the Lord's holy table, they give the people their mass — a mockery of the true supper of the Lord. They have bewitched the minds of simple people, brought them from true worship into idolatry, making the bread and wine into

Christ our Lord and Savior, even though Christ said, "Do this in remembrance of me."

Instead of prayers in English, these thieves give the people prayers in a language they cannot understand, preventing them from praying together with the priest. Paul called praying in a strange tongue barbarous, childish, unprofitable folly, and plain madness.

Instead of godly articles of unity in religion and wholesome sermons, these thieves provide the Pope's laws and decrees, lying legends, feigned fables and miracles.

I cannot consent to this robbery, because it is blasphemy against God, high treason against Christ. It is plainly against God's Word and Christ's gospel, against my salvation and that of my brothers and sisters, which Christ so dearly bought for us all. This is why I am being put to death, which I willingly accept, sure that I will receive everlasting life in return.

These thieves are worse than a thief who robs and kills the body, for these kill both body and soul. These church robbers so disguise their spiritual robbery that they can make people believe that lies are truth and truth is a lie; light is darkness, and darkness light; evil good and good evil; superstition true religion and idolatry true worship.

These robbers cannot be fought as common robbers are, with spears and lances. Our weapons must be spiritual and heavenly. We must fight them with the armor of God, not intending to kill their bodies but their errors, their heresies, idolatries, superstitions, and hypocrisy, in an attempt to save both their bodies and their souls. Our weapons are faith, hope, charity, righteousness, truth, patience, and prayer; our sword is the Word of God. With these weapons, we will win by never yielding to the enemy, even though we are murdered like sheep. The crueler and more painful our deaths, the more glorious they are in God and the more blessed our martyrdom.

I tell you this so you won't be ashamed by my death. If you love me, you will rejoice that God has called me to this honor, which is greater than any earthly honor I could ever attain. Who wouldn't be happy to die for this cause? I trust in my Lord God, who put His mind, will, and affection in my heart, and choose to lose all my worldly substance, and my life, too, rather than deny His known truth. He will comfort me, aid me, and strengthen me forever, even to the yielding of my spirit and soul into His hands. I most heartily beg His infinite goodness and mercy, through Christ our Lord. Amen.

9

Archbishop Cranmer

Thomas Cranmer came from an ancient family dating back to the conquest. He was born in Arselacton, Nottinghamshire, brought up in schools from the time he was an infant, and attended the University of Cambridge, where he received his master of arts and was made a professor of Jesus College. When he married a gentleman's daughter, he gave up his fellowship at Cambridge and became the reader at Buckingham College.

Cranmer's wife died in childbirth and he returned to Cambridge where, as a doctor of divinity, he became one of those who examined students before they were granted their bachelors or doctorates. Since he strongly believed that students of divinity should know Scripture, that knowledge became one of the prerequisites for graduation. This meant that some friars and monks who were educated in the study of Church authors and knew little Scripture were denied degrees and disliked Cranmer, although some took the time to study the Bible and were successful.

Because of his reputation as a scholar, Cranmer was offered a position in Cardinal Wolsey's new college at Oxford, which he turned down. About this time Cardinal Campegio and Cardinal Wolsey had been appointed by the Pope to decide the case between Henry VIII and his wife. They delayed the proceedings all that summer and adjourned in August, saying it was against the law to decide ecclesiastical matters during the harvest, since this was a decision no one really wanted to be responsible for. Furious at the delay, Henry ordered Campegio to return to Rome.

Two of the king's advisors happened to spend a night in the same house in Waltham where Cranmer was staying to avoid the plague that was sweeping through Cambridge, and the three of them met at supper, where Cranmer was asked for his opinion on the king's divorce and remarriage.

Cranmer replied that he hadn't studied the matter but thought they were spending too much time prosecuting the ecclesiastical law. He thought the question should be decided according to the Bible. This would satisfy Henry, instead of dragging the decision out from year to year, since the learned men of England could easily find the answer in the Bible.

The two men thought that was a good idea and said they would mention it to the king, which they did the next day.

"Where is this Dr. Cranmer?" the king asked. "Is he still at Waltham?"

They said he was there when they left that morning.

"I want to speak with him. Send for him. I think that man has the sow by the right ear. If I'd known about this two years ago, it could have saved me a great deal of money and eased my mind."

Cranmer didn't want to go to the king, saying he hadn't studied the matter thoroughly enough, but eventually he had no choice but to appear at the king's court.

"I think you have the right idea," the king told Cranmer. "You must understand that my conscience has bothered me for a long time, and this could relieve it one way or another. I command you to see my cause furthered as much as you can. I don't want to be divorced from the queen if our marriage is not against God's laws. No prince ever had a more gentle, obedient, and loving companion than my wife. If this doubt hadn't arisen, I would be content to stay with her, as long as it is in the will and pleasure of Almighty God."

Cranmer said it would be a good idea to have the matter examined by the best men of Cambridge and Oxford, according to the Bible.

"That's fine. But I also want you to write your opinion," the king agreed, ordering the Earl of Wiltshire to put Cranmer up in his house at Durham Place while he studied the matter. Cranmer's decision was that the Pope had no authority to dispense with the Word of God and the Scriptures.

"Will you stand by this before the Bishop of Rome?" Henry asked him.

"I will, by God's grace, if your majesty sends me there," Cranmer replied.

Through Cranmer, learned men were sent to most of the universities in Christendom to discuss the question, as well as at Oxford and Cambridge. The decision was that Henry's marriage to his brother's wife was unlawful according to God's Word and they should be divorced. A delegation was sent to Rome to meet with the Pope: the Earl of Wiltshire, Dr. Cranmer, Dr. Stokesley, Dr. Carne, Dr. Bennet, and others.

When the time came for them to see the Pope, he sat in his rich apparel with sandals on his feet, which he offered to be kissed by the ambassadors. The Earl of Wiltshire made no move to kiss the Pope's feet, so no one else did, either. They offered to defend their belief that no man could legally marry his brother's wife and that the Pope could not provide a dispensation for this infraction of God's law. Although the delegation was promised time to discuss the matter with the Pope, they were dismissed without ever seeing him again.

Everyone but Cranmer returned to England, while he went to the emperor's council to support the divorce, receiving no argument on the point from them.

At the time of the passing of the Six Articles, Cranmer stood against the whole parliament for three days, arguing against their passage, until Henry ordered him to leave the chamber so the act could be passed.

When Lord Cromwell was arrested and the Catholics thought everything was going their way, they appointed ten or twelve bishops to go to Cranmer and convince him to support several new laws about religion. Even those he trusted — Bishop Heath and Bishop Skip — urged him to yield to what they thought was Henry's will on these matters, but Cranmer refused. Instead, he went to the king, argued against the proposed regulations, won him over, and the laws were not passed.

Not long after, the Bishop of Winchester and others told Henry that Cranmer was stirring the people up with his ideas and should be examined for heresy. Henry reluctantly agreed, telling Cranmer the news himself.

When he heard that he was to be tried for heresy, Cranmer replied, "I most humbly thank your highness, for there are those who have slandered me, and I hope to prove myself innocent."

"Don't you know how many enemies you have?" Henry asked. "Think how easy it would be to find three or four liars to witness against you. Do you think you'll have any better luck than your master, Christ, did? You would run headlong to your death, if I let you!

"Tomorrow, when the council sends for you, go to them. If they commit you to the Tower, ask to have your accusers brought before you without being imprisoned. You're a member of the council, and that's your right. If they insist on imprisoning you, give them my ring and appeal to me. As soon as they see my ring, they'll know I have agreed to take over the matter and have dismissed them."

The following day Cranmer answered as the king had instructed him. Deciding that no persuasion of his would keep him out of prison, he appealed to the king and delivered the ring to them. Somewhat amazed, the whole council immediately rose and took the king his ring, surrendering the matter into his hands.

The king addressed the council. "Ah, my lords, I thought I had wiser men in my council. I was content that you try him as a councillor, not as a common subject, but now I see you would have treated him harshly. If a prince can be beholden to a subject, I am most beholden to my lord Canterbury."

Cranmer's enemies decided they had to ruin his good reputation with the king before proceeding against him. They arranged to have him accused of preaching erroneous doctrine by the clerics of his own cathedral and the most famous justices of the peace in the county, then delivered the charges to the king.

Henry read the charges, put them in his shirt, and then went for a ride on the Thames to calm down. Seeing Cranmer on the shore at Lambeth bridge, he asked him to come aboard for a talk. "I have news from Kent for you," the king began.

"Good, I hope," Cranmer replied.

"So good that I now know the greatest heretic in Kent." Henry pulled out the charges against Cranmer, giving them to him for reading.

Cranmer was deeply hurt to see those he thought were his friends accusing him, but asked the king to appoint a commission to look into the charges.

"I intend to," the king said. "And you will be the chief commissioner, along with two or three others you appoint."

"People will say the commission isn't impartial if I judge myself," Cranmer protested.

Within three weeks it was obvious that the charges were a Catholic plot against Cranmer. The king told him to appoint twelve or sixteen men to search the houses and persons of those in the plot and bring anything they found to him. In less than four hours of searching, the conspiracy was brought to light by the seizure of letters from the Bishop of Winchester and others.

Two of the men involved were especially good friends of Cranmer: the suffragan bishop of Dover and Dr. Barber, a layman. One day Cranmer called them both into his study. "I need some good advice from you," he began. "One or two men whom I trusted have disclosed my secrets and accused me of heresy. How should I behave toward them? You're both my friends, and I have always talked to you when I needed advice. What do you think?"

"Such villains should be hung!" Dr. Barber replied.

"Hanging's too good for them! I would hang them myself!" said the suffragan.

Cranmer threw his hands up toward heaven. "O Lord, most merciful God," he called, "who can a man trust these days?" Pulling the letters out, he asked, "Do you know these letters?"

The two men fell on their knees, begging forgiveness, saying they had been tempted to write the letters by others.

"Well," said Cranmer, "God make you both good men. I never deserved this at your hands, but you should ask God's forgiveness. If I can't trust you, what should I do? I see now that there is no trust among men. I even fear my left hand will accuse my right hand. This shouldn't surprise me, for our Savior Jesus Christ warned that such a world would come in the last days. I beseech Him of His great mercy to finish that time shortly."

This was the last attempt made against Cranmer during the days of Henry VIII. Under Edward VI, Cranmer's influence was even greater (he was the young king's godfather). It was during Edward's reign that Cranmer had discussions with Bishop Ridley that confirmed his views of theology. He took on the defense of the entire Protestant doctrine regarding the idolatry of the mass, writing five books for the Church of England on the subject.

At sixteen, King Edward fell sick and bequeathed the throne to Lady Jane Grey, King Henry's niece, not wanting his sister Mary, who was a Catholic, to have the throne. All the nobles agreed, then sent for Cranmer and asked if he would join them in supporting Lady Jane, but Cranmer refused. He had taken an oath to abide by Henry's will, which specified Mary, not Lady Jane Grey. Cranmer talked to Edward about the matter and was assured that Lady Jane could legally have the throne. Once he discussed it with some lawyers, Cranmer, too, agreed.

On Edward's death, the lords commanded that Lady Jane should take the throne, even though she was unwilling to be queen. This was opposed by the House of Commons — not because it favored Mary but because it hated some of Lady Jane's supporters. With their support, Mary took the throne, came to London, and beheaded Lady Jane when she refused to worship as a Catholic.

The nobles who had supported Lady Jane were required to pay a fine and were forgiven, except for the dukes of Northumberland and Suffolk and Archbishop Cranmer. He desired a pardon, but Mary refused to see him because of the role he had played in Henry's divorce from her mother. She also held Cranmer responsible for Protestantism being accepted in Edward's reign.

Soon a rumor was spread around that Cranmer had offered to say a mass at Edward's funeral, hoping to find favor with Mary. He immediately denied the rumor, stating his feelings about the mass in a letter that someone made public. Cranmer was ordered to appear before the commissioners. Although he was allowed to leave the hearing at that time, he was soon arrested, imprisoned in the Tower, and condemned for treason.

The queen realized that she had pardoned everyone else from Edward's time and that Cranmer had supported her longer than anyone else when Edward wanted to give the throne to Lady Jane, so she pardoned him from treason but let the charges of heresy stand.

In time Cranmer was transferred to Oxford to dispute his theology with the doctors and divines there. Now the queen and her bishops had already decided what would happen to Cranmer, but the dispute would serve to cover his murder.

On September 12, 1555, Cranmer appeared before Bishop Brooks, Dr. Martin, Dr. Story, the queen's commissioners, and a number of other officials at St. Mary. Brought before the panel, Cranmer took off his cap and bowed to the queen's commissioners one at a time. Then, looking the Pope's representative in the eye, he put his cap back on and stood straight, refusing to accept his authority.

"This I do profess concerning my faith," Cranmer began. "I want you to note that I will never agree that the Bishop of Rome has any jurisdiction in this country. I made an oath to the king, and no foreign person is above him. The Pope is contrary to the crown, and I cannot serve both.

"The Bishop of Rome is also against God's laws, which set aside one day a week for church, so all people should hear God's laws in their own tongue and understand them. But the Pope commands the service to be said in Latin, which no one understands. God would have it otherwise.

"Concerning the sacrament, I have taught no false doctrine. If it can be proved by any doctor that Christ's body is really present there, I will submit.

"Christ commands all to drink of the cup; the Pope takes it away from the laymen. Christ tells us to obey the king; the Pope tells us to obey him. If I obey him, I cannot obey Christ.

"Christ said the antichrist will appear. Who shall he be? One that advances himself above all other creatures. Until someone advances himself more than the Pope does, let him be the antichrist."

After Cranmer's speech, he answered the charges against him.

- *Before he entered holy orders, he had married Joan Black or Brown, from Cambridge.*

Cranmer said he had married Joan, but wasn't sure if her name was Black or Brown.

- *After her death he took holy orders and was made an archbishop by the Pope.*

Cranmer said he'd received a letter from the Pope that he delivered to the king, and the king made him an archbishop.

* *Being in holy orders, he married a woman named Anne.*

That was true, Cranmer said.

* *During Henry VIII's reign, he kept his wife secretly and had children.*

Cranmer said that was true. It was better to have his own wife than do as other priests did and steal other men's wives.

* *During Edward's time, he lived openly with his wife.*

Cranmer said he did, because the laws of England said he could.

* *That he was not ashamed of his wife.*

He had no reason to be ashamed of her, he said.

* *That he refused the authority of the Church, held the heresy concerning the sacrament of the altar, and published his beliefs.*

Cranmer agreed he had written the books the panel named.

* *That he compelled others, against their wills, to agree with him.*

He exhorted those who agreed, but compelled no one to agree.

* *Since he would not stop perpetuating such enormous crimes, he was locked in the Tower.*

Cranmer replied that he knew of no enormous crimes he'd committed.

* *That he was convicted of heresy in Oxford.*

Cranmer admitted he was denounced but maintained he was not a heretic.

- *He left the Catholic Church and moved the king and his subjects to do the same.*

Cranmer admitted he had left the Pope, but said there was no schism in it.

- *That he had twice been sworn to the Pope.*

He replied that he had obeyed the laws of the country when he did so.

- *That he usurped the power of the Pope by consecrating bishops and priests.*

Cranmer said he did consecrate bishops and priests, but the laws of the land had given him that power.

- *That although the whole country submitted to the authority of the Pope, he would not.*

Cranmer agreed that he would not submit to the Pope, but said he was correct in not doing so.

On February 14, 1555, Cranmer was recalled before a new commission, condemned, stripped of his Church offices, and turned over to the secular authorities.

By now Cranmer had been in prison for almost three years. The doctors and divines of Oxford all tried to make him recant, even allowing him to stay in the dean's house while they argued with him, and eventually Cranmer gave in to their requests and signed a recantation accepting the Pope's authority in all things. The queen was delighted with his recantation but still determined that Cranmer would die. He remained in prison.

Cranmer was miserable, not being able to die honestly or live dishonestly. In the meantime, Queen Mary secretly told Dr. Cole to prepare a funeral sermon for Cranmer's burning on March 21. On March 20, Dole went to Cranmer to see if he was standing by his recantation. Assured that he was, Cole returned early on March 21 to give Cranmer some money for the poor. Cranmer realized what was about to happen to him. A Spanish friar came in to ask him to write his recantation out twice with his own hand and sign it, which he did, then Cranmer wrote a prayer and sermon that he secretly tucked into his shirt, and waited.

Since it was a cold, rainy day, Cranmer was brought into St. Mary's Church with all the nobles, justices, and the crowd that had gathered. Dr. Cole gave his sermon, saying that although Cranmer had repented of his errors, the queen had other reasons for sending him to his death. He commended Cranmer for his works, saying he was unworthy of death but that masses would be said for his soul in all the churches of Oxford. Then Cole asked Cranmer to read his profession of faith, so everyone would see he was a good Catholic.

Cranmer's prayers and confession of faith were well within the doctrine of the Catholic Church until the very end, when he said, "And now I come to the great thing that troubles my conscience more than anything I ever did or said in my whole life, and that is the publishing of a writing contrary to the truth, which now here I renounce and refuse, as things written by my hand contrary to the truth I believed with my whole heart, written because I feared death. Since my hand offended, it will be punished: When I come to the fire, it first will be burned. As for the Pope, I refuse him, as Christ's enemy and antichrist, with all his false doctrine. And as for the sacrament, I believe as I have taught in my book...."

The congregation was amazed at Cranmer's words, and the Catholic churchmen there raged, fretted, and fumed because they had nothing left to threaten him with. He could only die once, after all.

When he came to the place where Hugh Latimer and Ridley had been burned before him, Cranmer knelt down briefly to pray, then undressed to his shirt, which hung down to his bare feet. His head, once he took off his caps, was so bare there wasn't a hair on it. His beard was long and thick, covering his face, which was so grave it moved both his friends and enemies.

As the fire approached him, Cranmer put his right hand into the flames, keeping it there until everyone could see it burned before his body was touched. "This unworthy right hand!" he called out often before he gave up the ghost.

10

Gertrude Crokhay

Gertrude Crokhay lived with her second husband in St.
Katherine's parish, near the Tower of London. In 1558, a child
portraying St. Nicholas made his way around the parish, but
Gertrude refused to let him into her house. The next day Dr.
Mallet and twenty others appeared at her door to ask why she
wouldn't let St. Nicholas in and receive his blessing.

"Sir," she answered, "I didn't know St. Nicholas came
here."

"Yes," said the doctor. "Here's the boy who played him."

"My neighbor's child was here, but not St. Nicholas, for St.
Nicholas is in heaven. I was afraid he would steal from me,
because I'd heard of men robbed by St. Nicholas's clerks." Dr.
Mallet left Gertrude, not able to trap her into saying anything
that could be construed as heresy.

In 1559, Gertrude served as godmother for a child being
baptized in the Catholic Church after it had secretly been
baptized with the Protestant service. When her enemies heard
of this, they began looking for her, but she had gone across the
sea to Guelderland to see some land that had been left to her
children by her first husband. After three months, she started
home by way of Antwerp. She was seen there by John Johnson,
a Dutchman who was fighting with her husband over a bill. He

accused her of being an Anabaptist and had her imprisoned to get even with her husband.

Gertrude remained in prison for two weeks, during which she saw some prisoners secretly drowned in wine vats and cast into the river. She expected the same would eventually be done to her, and in her fear she came down with the sickness that later killed her.

Finally called to be tried as an Anabaptist, Gertrude declared her faith so boldly in Dutch that she was released from prison and allowed to return to England.

The Spurges, Cavill, Ambrose, Drake, and Tims

These six men lived in the county of Essex. Being accused of heresy, they were all arrested and sent up to Bishop Gardiner of London, who sent the first four to Marshalsea Prison and the last two to the King's Bench.

After having been confined for a year, they were all brought into the court at St. Paul's Church to be examined by Bishop Bonner. Bonner began his examination with Tims, whom he called the ringleader, telling him he had taught the others heresies and made them as guilty as himself. After talking this way for a while, the bishop asked Tims to submit himself to the Church.

In answer to this, Tims reminded the bishop that he himself had formerly given up the very church he now professed such a love for during the reign of Henry VIII. "My lord, that which you have written against the supremacy of the Pope can be proved true by Scripture. What you are doing now is contrary to the Word of God, as I can show." At this, Bonner called Tims an obstinate heretic and condemned him.

Drake's trial came next. He frankly declared that he denied the authority of the Pope and no persuasion would change his mind. No time was wasted in condemning Drake and turning him over to the secular authorities for punishment. The four remaining prisoners, Thomas and Richard Spurg, George Ambrose, and John Cavill, were then asked if they would forsake their heresies and return to the Church. They all refused to acknowledge any wrongdoing and declined to change their beliefs.

On April 14, 1556, the six men were taken to Smithfield, where they were chained to the same stake and burned in one fire. They patiently submitted themselves to the flames and quietly resigned their souls to that Redeemer for whose sake they had given their bodies to be burned.

Hugh Laverock and John Apprice

Hugh Laverock was a painter by trade, living in the parish of Barking, Essex. At the time of his arrest he was sixty-eight years old and very infirm. Being accused of heresy by some of his neighbors, he and John Apprice, a poor blind man, were taken before Bonner to be examined.

Bonner asked the prisoners the usual questions, to which they answered without making the slightest effort to conceal their opinions. One week after they had been sentenced, they were taken to Stratford-le-Bow, the place appointed for their execution. As soon as they arrived at the stake, Laverock threw away his crutch and spoke to Apprice. "Be of good comfort, brother, for the bishop of London is our good physician. He will cure us both shortly, you of your blindness and me of my lameness." Then they both knelt down and prayed earnestly that God would enable them to pass with

Christian resolution through the fiery trial. These two poor old men — one a cripple and the other blind — were then chained to one stake and the fagots lighted. They endured their sufferings with great fortitude and cheerfully yielded up their lives for their faith.

Catherine Hut, Joan Hornes & Elizabeth Thackvill

These three women were arrested on suspicion of heresy and taken before Sir John Mordaunt and Mr. Tyrrel, justices of the peace for the county of Essex. After a hearing they were sent as prisoners to the Bishop of London for refusing to attend the services of the Catholic Church.

The three prisoners were brought before the bishop and asked the normal questions, to which they replied that they believed in the reformed faith. Refusing to recant, they were sentenced to be burned and were delivered to the sheriff of London, who put them in Newgate Prison until their execution. On the appointed day, they were carried to Smithfield, fastened to one stake, and burned together for their faith.

The Thirteen

Thirteen people who lived in the county of Essex were arrested in May, 1556, and sent to London to be examined by Bishop Bonner: Ralph Jackson, Henry Adlington, Lyon Cawch, William Halliwell, George Searles, John Routh, John Derifall, Henry Wye, Edmund Hurst, Lawrence Parnam, Thomas Bower, Elizabeth Pepper, and Agnes George.

On the Sunday after their condemnation, Dr. Fecknam, dean of St. Paul's, said that the thirteen "held as many different beliefs as there were faces among them." This being reported to them, they drew up one confession of faith that they all signed. Early on the morning of June 28, 1556, all thirteen were taken from Newgate to Stratford-le-Bow, where the sheriff separated them into two groups and told each group that the other had recanted. When he found this strategy wouldn't work, he continued with the execution.

The eleven men were tied to three stakes, but the two women were in the middle, not tied to any stake. All burned together in one fire.

Julius Palmer

Julius Palmer was the son of a merchant living in the city of Coventry. He received his early education at the public school there and was sent to Oxford, where he was graduated and elected a fellow of Magdalene College.

Palmer had been brought up as a Catholic, and he refused to conform to the religious changes made during Edward VI's time, so he was expelled from the college and served as a schoolteacher in the town of Oxford. When Queen Mary came to power, Palmer was returned to his post at the college. But while he had been away from the college, Palmer had made the acquaintance of several leaders of the reform party and began to doubt whether it was necessary to obey the Pope in order to be a good Christian. When the persecution began, he began to look into the cases of those arrested and how they behaved themselves through the whole process of condemnation and burning, even sending one of his pupils to report back to him on the burning of Bishop Hooper.

Before this, Palmer was inclined to think that very few men would brave the fire for the sake of their religion, but when he heard of Hooper's heroism and attended the examination of Ridley and Latimer, he totally changed his mind. From then on, he studied the Scriptures thoroughly and became a zealous reformer.

Palmer began to miss mass and other church ceremonies, which brought enough suspicion on him that he felt he should leave the college. He accepted a post as a grammar-school teacher in Reading, Berkshire until driven out of there by enemies who threatened to turn him in for his Protestant beliefs.

Entirely destitute, Palmer went to his mother, hoping to obtain the legacy his father had left him four years before. But his mother was a heartless, bigoted woman who hated the reformers and was afraid of being accused of harboring a heretic. As soon as she saw him standing at her door, she motioned him away: "Get thee gone, heretic! Get thee gone!" she exclaimed.

"Mother, I don't deserve this!" Palmer replied.

"You have been banished from Oxford and Reading as a heretic."

Nothing Palmer could say would change his mother's mind, so he decided to travel to Reading in hopes of getting his back pay there, but was arrested and thrown into prison with Thomas Askine and John Gwin. After standing firm at their trials, all three were condemned as heretics.

While in prison awaiting their execution, Palmer comforted his two fellow-sufferers and urged them to hold onto the faith they professed. When the fire was kindled and began to take hold on the bodies of the three martyrs, they lifted up their hands toward heaven and cried out, "Lord, strengthen us! Lord, receive our souls!" And so they continued without any struggle, holding up their hands and calling on the Lord, until they died.

Joan Waste

This poor woman, having become a convert to the reformed faith, bought a New Testament and paid a small sum daily to an old man who came and read it to her, since she was blind. By this means and through her unusual memory, she became so familiar with the Bible that she could repeat entire chapters by heart. When she refused to attend services in the Catholic Church, Joan was brought before Dr. Ralph Bayn, Bishop of Litchfield and Coventry, and Dr. Draycott, the chancellor, charged with heresy, and committed to the prison of Derby.

She was examined several times by Peter Finch, the bishop's official, and afterwards brought to public examination before the bishop, his chancellor, and several of the queen's commissioners. The poor woman answered that she could not forsake the truth and begged them to cease troubling her. Finding that she would say nothing else, the sentence of death was finally pronounced and she was handed over to the sheriff. On August 1, 1556, she was led to the stake. As soon as she came to it, she kneeled down and repeated a prayer, desiring the spectators to pray for her. Having finished, she arose and was fastened to the stake, and when the fagots were lighted, the flames soon took away her speech and her life.

Alice Bendon

Alice Bendon was the wife of Edward Bendon, of the parish of Stablehurst, Kent. Being brought before a magistrate and charged with heresy, she was asked why she did not go to church. "Because there was so much idolatry practiced there," she replied. For this answer she was sent to Canterbury Castle. When her husband begged the Bishop of Dover to release her, he did, on the condition that she return to the Church. Despite her husband's appeals that she attend church with him, Alice continued to stay away from services and was rearrested and imprisoned. She remained there for nine weeks without any visitors, lying in her clothes on straw and having only a little bread and water every day. She soon became so weak and sick that she could barely walk, but was given slightly better treatment after her first visit with the bishop.

Alice and six others were brought before the commissioners at the end of the following April. Since they all held to their faith, they were sentenced and handed over to the sheriff for punishment. Alice Bendon bore herself with remarkable courage before the stake, yielding up her life with scarcely a struggle.

Richard Woodman

Woodman's parish priest, a man named Fairbank, had tried without success to convince Woodman to attend church services. Annoyed by his failure, Fairbank preferred charges of heresy against Woodman and had him brought before the justices of the peace for the county of Sussex, who committed him to the King's Bench prison for a considerable amount of time.

At length Woodman and four others were brought to be examined by Bishop Bonner of London, who advised them that they should become members of the true church. They answered that they considered themselves members of the church, and Bonner, satisfied with their replies, set all five men free.

Not long after Woodman returned home, the rumor was spread that he had joined the Catholic Church. He denied this so often and so publicly that a warrant was issued for his arrest. Three men approached Woodman one day as he worked in his father's warehouse, telling him he had to go with them before the lord chamberlain. Surprised and alarmed at this sudden attack, Woodman begged to be allowed to go home to tell his wife of the arrest and dress properly for court. The officers agreed to this and accompanied Woodman to his home. Once there, Woodman asked to see their warrant.

"It's not here," one of them replied. "It's at my house. The most you can do is make me go get it."

"If you have a warrant, fetch it," Woodman demanded. "Until you do have it, leave my house." He then shut the door in their faces. Knowing they would soon return, Woodman ran to a window in the rear of the house and escaped to a nearby forest, where he hid himself. The officers soon came back with the warrant and searched the house from top to bottom, but Woodman was safe in the woods.

Woodman knew they would search the whole country for him, including the seacoast, and it would be impossible for him to leave the country, so he decided the best thing to do would be to stay close to home, which no one would even think of. Bringing out his Bible, pen, ink, and other necessities, Woodman hid under a tree in the nearby woods for six or seven weeks. His wife brought him food every day. At last there was a report that he had been seen in Flanders, and the local search was given up. Woodman took the opportunity to escape to Flanders and France, but he missed his home and family too much to stay and sneaked back into the country. Within three weeks, another warrant was issued for his arrest, and his house was searched as often as twice a week for the next two months.

In the end, Woodman was betrayed by his own brother, who told the authorities that he left his hiding place in the evening to sleep at home. When the authorities came to his house, Woodman hid in a secret loft that had never been discovered in all of the previous searches. Although they knew he had to be somewhere in the house, the officers couldn't find him anywhere. Woodman's brother knew the loft existed, but he didn't know exactly where it was, so the search was renewed until one of them finally spotted the loft, forcing Woodman to make a run for it.

"As soon as I found myself on the ground, I started and ran down a lane that was full of sharp cinders, and the men came running after me," Woodman said. "I turned about hastily to go on, when I stepped upon a sharp stone with one foot, and in trying to save it I slipped into a great miry hole, and fell down, and before I could arise and get away they were upon me. Then they bound me and took me away."

Woodman was taken to London and examined by several church officials, but refused to yield to anything that was not founded on the Bible's authority. About two weeks after being sentenced, Woodman was taken to the town of Lewes, in Sussex, with nine other prisoners. On July 22, 1557, the ten men were led to the place of execution. There they were chained to several stakes and consumed in one great fire. It is recorded that they all went to their deaths with wonderful courage and resignation, with their last words committing their souls to that blessed Redeemer who was to be their final judge.

John Hullier

John Hullier came from a respectable family and was sent to Eton and King's College, Cambridge, where he devoted himself to the study of theology, intending to become a minister. After he graduated, he became the curate at Babram, a village about three miles from Cambridge. He hadn't been there long before he went to Lynn, where he had some dispute with the authorities. They reported Hullier's sayings to Dr. Thurlby, bishop of the diocese, who sent for him and, after a short examination, committed him to the castle of Cambridge.

A short time after this he was called to appear at St. Mary's Church before several doctors of law and divinity, by whom he was reproved. His examination being finished, he was ordered to recant what they called his erroneous opinions. This he refused to do. Without any loss of time, he was degraded, condemned, and delivered over to the sheriff, who immediately seized all his books, papers, and writings.

On the day appointed for Hullier's execution, he was led to the stake outside the town. He called on the spectators to pray for him and to bear witness that he died for the truth. One of the proctors of the university and some of the fellows of Trinity college were displeased at his addressing the people and reproved the mayor for allowing him to speak. Hullier took no notice of this, but being chained to the stake, he earnestly prayed to be strengthened to undergo the fiery trail. As soon as the fagots were lit, a number of his books were thrown into the midst of the flames, among them a communion book that Hullier caught joyfully and held in his hand and looked at as long as he could.

John Hullier's death was greatly lamented by many of the people, who prayed for him and showed their sorrow by tears, he having been a kind and charitable man.

Simon Miller & Elizabeth Cooper

Simon Miller was a prosperous merchant of the town of Lynn-Regis. He was an earnest supporter of the reformers' doctrines, and having occasion to go to Norwich on business, he inquired while there for a place of worship. This being reported to chancellor Dunning, he ordered Miller to appear before him. When the chancellor asked him the usual questions, Miller answered without attempting to hide his thoughts on the subject of religion, so he was committed to the bishop's palace as a prisoner.

After spending some time in prison, Miller was allowed to go home to settle his affairs. On his return he was again examined by the chancellor, who warned him to recant and return to the Catholic Church, but Miller remained firm in his faith and was condemned as a heretic.

Elizabeth Cooper, who was burned with Simon Miller, was the wife of a tradesman in Norwich. She had formerly been persuaded to recant, but her conscience bothered her so that one day she went to St. Andrew's Church and withdrew her recantation in the presence of a large congregation. For this she was immediately arrested and sent to prison. The next day she was brought before the bishop and examined. This time she remained true to her faith and was condemned as a relapsed heretic.

On July 30, 1557, Simon Miller and Elizabeth Cooper were both led to the stake, which was set up in a field outside Norwich, near Bishopsgate. When the fire was lit, Elizabeth

Cooper was afraid, and cried out. Miller put his hand out toward her, telling her to be strong and of good cheer, "for, good sister," he said, "we shall have a joyful meeting hereafter." Upon hearing Miller's words, the woman seemed reassured and stood still and quiet until they both committed their souls to Almighty God and ended their lives.

A Woman at Norwich

Cicely Ormes, of the city of Norwich, wife of Edmund Ormes, was arrested on the day that Simon Miller and Elizabeth Cooper were executed. She drew the attention of the officers to herself by speaking encouraging words to the two prisoners on the way to the stake. For this she was put in prison and soon after taken before the chancellor for examination.

The chancellor offered to release her "if she would go to church and keep her beliefs to herself," and told her "she could hold to any faith she would."

But she answered, "I will not enter your church."

Then the chancellor told her he had shown more favor to her than he ever did to any person, and he didn't want to condemn her because she was only a foolish young woman.

Cicely replied that if she was only a foolish young woman, he shouldn't be worried about her belief. Foolish or not, she was content to give up her life for a cause so good.

The chancellor then read the sentence of condemnation and delivered Cicely Ormes to the care of the sheriffs of the city. Cicely was a young woman in the prime of life, uneducated, but very earnest in her cause. She was born in East Dereham and was the daughter of Thomas Haund, a tailor. The first time she was brought before the magistrate she recanted, but was afterward so troubled by her conscience that she wrote a letter to the chancellor to let him know she repented of her action. But before the letter could be delivered, she was arrested, tried, and convicted.

Cicely Ormes was burned on September 23, 1557, between seven and eight in the morning. When she came to the stake, she kneeled down and made her prayers to God. That being done, she rose up and said, "Good people, I believe as I have been taught from the Bible. This I do, and I will never change my mind. My death is a witness of my faith to all present here. Good people, as many of you as believe the same as I do, pray for me." When she had said this, she laid her hand on the stake and saw it was black — she was burned at the same stake as Simon Miller and Elizabeth Cooper — and wiped it on her dress. After she had been bound and the fire was lit, she clasped her hands together against her heart, turning her face upward, and raised her lands little by little, until they fell helpless at her side when she died.

William Munt, Alice, Rose Allen

William Munt, his wife, Alice, and his daughter, Rose Allen, lived near the town of Colchester, not far from London. They had become converted and thought it was wrong to attend the services held in the local Catholic Church, although they were warned this was a dangerous breaking of the queen's laws. Still, their sense of duty was stronger than their fears, and they continued to worship in secret places in their own way, with a few men and women of like faith, until they were turned in by Sir Thomas Tye.

The family was forced to flee the area for several months, but returned to their house when the issue died down locally.

A few days later, Edmund Tyrrel, a bailiff, two constables, and a large number of people came to their door at two o'clock in the morning to arrest them. The sudden alarm unnerved Mrs. Munt, who was not in good health. Feeling faint, she asked Tyrrel to let her daughter, Rose, go fetch her some water before they all left for prison.

Tyrrell permitted Rose to go out with her pitcher to the well, saying to her as she passed him, "Persuade your father and mother, girl, to bear themselves more like good Christians and less like heretics. Then they may soon go free."

"Sire," Rose replied to Tyrrel, "they have a better instructor than I am — One who, I hope, will not allow them to err."

"Well, it's time to lock up such heretics as you!" Tyrrel replied. Tyrrel took the candle from the girl, and holding her wrist in a firm grip, put the lighted candle under her hand, burning it across the back until the skin cracked. "Cry, wench! Let me hear you cry!" he yelled. Rose refused to utter a sound until Tyrrel threw her back into the house before taking them all to jail.

The same morning they also arrested six others: William Bongeor, Thomas Benhote, William Purchase, Agnes Silverside, Helen Ewing, and Elizabeth Folk. After they had been confined a few days, they were all brought before several justices of the peace, priests, and officers.

The first person called was William Bongeor, who being examined concerning his religion declared he was of the reformed faith. Thomas Benhote was next, and he also denied the authority of the Pope. William Purchase answered likewise. Agnes Silverside said she did not approve of the popish consecration or the pageantry and superstitions of the Catholic Church. Helen Ewring also renounced all the unscriptural doctrines and practices of the Catholic Church. The others answered with equal firmness, refusing to change their belief in any way. Finding them immovable, sentence was pronounced.

Bishop Bonner, as soon as he received an account of the trial, sent down a warrant for the burning of the ten convicted persons, fixing August 2, 1557, as the day of execution. Since the prisoners were confined in different places, it was arranged that some of them should be executed in the morning and others in the afternoon. Accordingly, William Bongeor, William Purchase, Thomas Benhote, Agnes Silverside, Helen Ewring, and Elizabeth Folk were brought early in the morning to the stake.

The stakes were set up on a level plot of ground just outside the town of Colchester. The six prisoners knelt down and made their prayers, then rose and made themselves ready for the fire. When all six were nailed to their stakes and the fire blazed up about them, the people who stood looking on — thousands of them — cried out, "Lord strengthen thee! Lord comfort thee!" and other words of comfort.

In the afternoon they brought out William Munt, John Johnson, Alice Munt, and Rose Allen. After the martyrs had made their prayers and were tied to the stakes, they gave themselves to the flames with such courage that the people who saw them wondered.

Mrs. Joyce Lewis

Mrs. Joyce Lewis came from an excellent family of Warwickshire. She had been well educated and was used to the society of refined, cultured people. Her husband, Thomas Lewis, was of the same county, and her equal in station, but a hard, selfish man.

Mrs. Lewis had been brought up a Catholic and attended church regularly, hearing mass, going to confession, and faithfully observing all the ceremonies of the church — until she was convinced of the truth of the reformed faith. Her conversion was brought about when she attended the burning of Laurence Saunders and asked advice of Glover, who told her to study the Scriptures and regulate her faith and conduct by them alone.

One day Mrs. Lewis attending services at the Catholic Church with her husband and expressed her disapproval of some of the ceremonies she saw there by turning her back on the altar. Several people noticed her action and reported her to the Bishop of Litchfield, who issued her a summons. When the officer appeared with the warrant, Mr. Lewis became so angry that he drew a dagger on the officer and forced him to destroy the summons before he would let him go.

The bishop immediately summoned both Mr. and Mrs. Lewis to appear before him. Mr. Lewis apologized for his actions and was set free. Mrs. Lewis was told she could go if she admitted she had done wrong in church, but she maintained that she had done the right thing and refused to apologize. Since she was an important person in town, the bishop gave Mrs. Lewis a month to think about it, setting her free on her husband's bond.

When the time for her trial had almost come, many of Mr. Lewis's friends advised him not to let her appear but to take her away and forfeit the bond. But Mr. Lewis worried more about his one-hundred-pound bond than he did about his wife and delivered her to the bishop, who sent her to prison.

Mrs. Lewis was examined several times by the bishop, who finally condemned her as a heretic and sentenced her to be burned. Mrs. Lewis was then sent back to prison, where she remained for another year.

When the time drew near for her death, Mrs. Lewis asked certain friends of hers to come to her cell so she could talk to them for the last time. The whole night before her execution, she was cheerful, if a little sad.

About eight in the morning, the sheriff came to the cell without warning. "Mistress Lewis, I am come to bring you tidings of the queen's command. You have but one hour more to live in this world. Prepare yourself."

"Master sheriff," Mrs. Lewis replied after a minute, "your message is welcome to me, and I thank God that He has thought me worthy to venture my life in His cause."

Mrs. Lewis was led through the town, a great crowd of people surrounding her, accompanied by two of her friends who stayed with her all the way to the stake. She was fastened to the stake with a chain, showing such cheerfulness and lack of fear that everyone present was deeply moved. When the fire was lit, she neither struggled nor stirred, but only lifted up her hands toward heaven, and was very soon dead, since the sheriff had seen to it that the wood was good and dry for her.

William Fetty

John Fetty, William's father, had been put in prison as a heretic because of information provided by his own wife. He was taken before Sir John Mordaunt, one of the queen's commissioners. After examination, he was sent to Lollards' Tower, where he was put in the stocks with a pitcher of water and a loaf of bread nearby, to show him that was the only food he could expect to receive.

Lollards' Tower was a large, detached room belonging to Bishop Bonner's palace, in London. It was used for the punishment and occasional torture of Protestants who were brought before the bishop accused of heresy. The most common punishments inflicted here were scourging and setting in the stocks, where some were fastened by their hands and others by their feet. They were generally permitted to sit on a stool, but to increase their punishment, some were given no seat. Lying with their backs on the ground was exceedingly exhausting and painful. In this dungeon, some were kept for several days and other for weeks, without any other food but bread and water. During all this time, they could have no visitors. Many of the prisoners died from their confinement in this tower.

After John Fetty had been in the Lollards' Tower for fifteen days, most of the time in the stocks, William came to the bishop's palace to obtain permission to see his father. When he arrived there, the bishop's chaplain asked what he wanted. Crying and looking sorrowfully toward the tower, the boy replied that he wanted to see his father. The chaplain asked who his father was, and when the boy told him the name, the chaplain said his father was a heretic and was being taught a lesson in the stocks.

The boy quickly replied, "My father is no heretic. You are a pack of murderers!"

At this, the angry chaplain seized the boy by the hand and dragged him to another room in the palace. After stripping him, he had him scourged in a most unmerciful manner, then taken to see his father with the blood running down to his heels.

As soon as the boy saw his father, he fell on his knees and showed him his wounds. The poor man exclaimed, "Who was this cruel to you?"

"I was looking for you," the boy told him, "when a murdering chaplain took me into the bishop's house and beat me."

One of the keepers overheard this. He grabbed the boy and dragged him back to the room where he had been beaten, where he was kept for three days with scarcely any food and beaten again. The father was also beaten for protesting their cruelty. At last the poor young prisoner became very weak from this inhuman treatment and Bonner gave orders to let him go. He also ordered the father to be brought before him early the next morning.

At first the bishop abused the father for his religious beliefs, but considering the trouble that might result from having beaten the boy, both father and son were set free. Unfortunately, the boy died a few days later from his wounds.

Alexander Gough and Alice Driver

Having heard that two people accused of heresy were in hiding near his house, justice Noone of Suffolk sent out his officers and took Alexander Gough, of Woodbridge, and Alice Driver of Grosborough. They put their prisoners in Melton jail, where after remaining a good while, they were at last taken to the town of Bury for examination.

Both the prisoners acknowledged their faith and were sent back to jail, where they remained for several months, and then were brought to Ipswich for their final hearing. It's said that the prisoners repeated their confession of faith there and firmly refused to save their lives by changing their religion.

They were both condemned to be burned and sent back to their prison to await their day of execution.

On November 4, 1557, very early in the morning, Alexander Gough and Alice Driver were taken from Melton jail to Ipswich, led by the sheriff and his officers and accompanied by a great crowd of people. They arrived at Ipswich about seven in the morning and were immediately led to the place of execution. When they reached the stake, they sang a hymn and knelt down to pray for some time. Becoming impatient, the sheriff ordered the bailiffs to interrupt their prayers.

Gough stood up and said to the sheriff, "Let us pray a little while longer, for we have a short time to live."

But the bailiff said, "Come on. Let's burn them!"

Gough answered, "Be careful, sheriff. If you forbid our prayers, the vengeance of God hangs over your head."

As they were being fastened to the stake and the iron chain was put around her neck, Alice Driver said, "Oh, here is a goodly handkerchief!"

Then some of their friends came and took the martyrs by the hands as they stood at the stake. Seeing this, the sheriff cried to his men, "Seize them! Don't let one of them escape." When the people heard the order and saw the danger those by the stake were in, they all ran toward it and crowded around the stake, hiding the friends of the martyrs.

When the sheriff saw that, he let them alone and arrested no one. Then fire was put to the wood, and amid its flames these two heroic spirits passed beyond the reach of man's cruelty.

Thomas Hudson

Thomas Hudson was a glover by trade, living in the town of Ailesham, in Norfolk. Although he had little schooling, he was a great student of the Scriptures and preached on Sundays to any of his neighbors who were interested in hearing the Bible read and explained.

When Queen Mary began her reign, all unlicensed ministers who publicly preached to the people became marked men. Hudson would have been among the first to be arrested and thrown into prison if he had not fled from his home. He traveled to Suffolk, and by constantly changing his lodgings from one house to another, escaped arrest.

But after a time Hudson's desire to see his wife and family became too strong to be resisted. In spite of the danger, he went home. Soon he heard that his enemies knew of his return, so he left his house and built a crude shelter beneath a pile of nearby firewood, only coming out in the darkness. This worked until the town's vicar threatened to burn Mrs. Hudson for hiding her husband. Hudson left his hiding place and openly walked into town, where he was arrested.

The bishop asked Hudson a great number of questions, all of which he answered honestly, and though he wasn't an educated man, Hudson's arguments were very strong. Finding he couldn't do anything with the man, the bishop finally condemned him and sent him to prison.

On May 19, 1558, Thomas Hudson was taken out of prison and led to a place called the Lollards' Pit, just outside the Bishop's gate at Norwich, along with two other condemned men. Just before the chain around him was made fast, Hudson stooped, slipped out from under the chain, and stood a little to one side. This caused many to wonder if he was about to recant, or if he was coming forward for his parents' blessing. But no one knew the real reason: Hudson had suddenly been afflicted with doubts and felt his faith growing weak. Therefore, not willing to die while feeling this way, he fell upon his knees and prayed to God, who sent him comfort. Then he rose with great joy, as a reborn man, and cried, "Now, thank God, I am strong, and care not what man can do unto me!" So going to the stake again, he put the chain around himself, and they were all burned together.

History of Bishop Bonner

Edmund Bonner, Bishop of London, who took so prominent a part in the persecution of the Protestants during Queen Mary's reign, was born at Hanley, in Worcestershire, about the year 1500. He was educated at Oxford, and having been admitted to the priesthood, entered the household of Cardinal Wolsey.

All through Henry's reign, Bonner appeared to be very earnest in his opposition to the Pope and strongly in favor of the Reformation. Upon Henry's death, however, he refused to take the oath of supremacy for Edward and was sent to prison until he agreed to be obedient to the new king, was released, and later imprisoned once again until Queen Mary took the throne.

Mary saw just what she needed in Bonner, who threw himself into the work of persecuting the Protestants with all his energy. It's said that two hundred of the martyrs of this time were personally tried and sentenced by him. Bonner was a harsh, persistent man, with no pity or compassion for the people brought before him. Nothing short of complete surrender would satisfy Bonner. So far did his rage against heresy carry him that he is said to have called for rods and beaten stubborn witnesses himself on several occasions.

When Elizabeth came to the throne, she singled Bonner out to mark with her disapproval, sending him to prison in her second year for refusing to accept her as the head of the Church of England. He remained there for ten years, dying in misery and wretchedness at the age of seventy. Although no one had seen Bonner for over ten years, his memory was so fresh and he was so hated by the people that he was buried at midnight to avoid a riot.

The Death of Queen Mary

After a long illness, Queen Mary died on November 17 at three or four in the morning, yielding her life to nature and her kingdom to her sister, Elizabeth.

Hearing her sighs before she died, her council asked if she was sad about the death of her husband. "Indeed, that may be one cause," the queen replied, "but that is not the greatest wound that pierces my oppressed mind."

No other king or queen of England spilled as much blood in a time of peace as Queen Mary did in four years through her hanging, beheading, burning, and imprisonment of good Christian Englishmen. When she first sought the crown and promised to retain the faith and religion of Edward, God went with her and brought her the throne through the efforts of the Protestants. But after she broke her promises to God and man, sided with Stephen Gardiner, and gave up her supremacy to the Pope, God left her. Nothing she did after that thrived.

Instead, she married King Philip and made England subject to a stranger. With Philip came the Pope and his mass, the monks and the nuns, but still, God prevented her from having her way.

No woman was ever more disappointed than Mary when she could not have children, even with the help of the Catholic Church's prayers. She seemed unable to win the favor of God, the hearts of her subjects, or the love of her husband.

At last, when nothing could sway her to stop the tyranny of her priests and spare her subjects who were being drawn daily as sheep to the slaughter, it pleased God to cut off her rule by death, giving her throne to another after she reigned for five years and five months.

I mention this unlucky reign of Queen Mary not to detract from her position, which she was called to by the Lord, but as a warning to men and women in authority who persecute Christ's Church and shed Christian blood, so they will not stumble on the same stone as the Jews who persecuted Christ and His Church, to their own destruction.

Queen Elizabeth

The death of Queen Mary seemed to dispel a black, gloomy cloud which for five years had hung like a pall over England. The crowning of Elizabeth was welcomed with joy by the Protestants, and their sufferings during the previous bloody reign were for a moment forgotten in the hope that better days had come.

But Elizabeth, Protestant and friend of the Reformation, loved power as much as her father, Henry VIII, and intended to be no less an absolute ruler of both church and state than he had been. Laws were speedily passed establishing Elizabeth as the supreme head of the church as well as the nation. She was empowered to create a high commission, or court, to try people accused of not taking part in the services of the established Church of England. The power of this court extended over the whole kingdom; the clergy as well as the people were subject to its rule. Any three members of this court could take measures to discover, by summoning witnesses or any other means, anyone who spoke against the queen's supremacy or refused to observe the forms of worship of the established church. They had the power to inquire into any heretical opinions that might be held, to look for seditious books or writings, to try all cases of wilful absence from services, and to punish the offenders by fines.

As can be seen, religious liberty, as we know it today, was almost as far as ever from being realized. More than a century would pass before persecution entirely ceased and the passage of a Toleration Act finally established complete freedom of worship in England. But at least Elizabeth was not cruel; aversion to bloodshed was as marked a feature of her character as the reverse had been in that of Mary. The dreadful fires continued for a while longer in Spain and the counties within her grasp, but with the ending of the reign of Queen Mary, the history of English martyrdom was brought to a close.

Index of Martyrs

A

Abbeys, James, 132
Abel, 74
Adlington, Henry, 178-79
Agapetus, 18
Alban, 18
Aless, 77
Allen, Rose, 188-90
Ambrose, George, 176-77
Andrew, 6-7
Anteros, 14
Appolonia, 15
Apprice, John, 177-78
Archinimus, 26
Askine, Thomas, 180
Attalus of Pergamos, 12

B

Babram, 43
Badby, John, 36-37
Barnes, Robert, 73-74
Bartholomew, 6
Bartlet, Robert, 46
Bendon, Alice, 181-82
Bennet, Thomas, 65-66
Bernard, Thomas, 46
Beveridge, Friar, 80
Bilney, Thomas, 59-61
Bland, John, 125-27
Blandina, 12

Bongeor, William, 189-90
Boniface, 26
Boughton, Joan, 43
Bower, Thomas, 178-79
Bradford, John, 119-24
Browne, John, 49-50
Burton, Edward, 142

C

Cardmaker, John, 108-109
Carver, Dirick, 128-31
Cassian, 22
Cavill, John, 176-77
Cawch, Lyon, 178-79
Chase, Thomas, 47
Clarke, Roger, 75-76
Clerk, Joan, 46
Clerk, John, 46
Cocker, William, 127
Constantinus, 15
Cooper, Elizabeth, 186-87
Cranmer, Thomas, 161-73
Crokhay, Gertrude, 175-76

D

Denley, John, 132-35
Derifall, John, 178-79
Didymus, 16
Dionysius, 15
Drake, 177
Driver, Alice, 194-95

E

Ewring, Helen, 189-90

F

Fabian, 15

Featherstone, 74

Felicitas, 13

Felix, Bishop of Rome, 18

Fetty, John, 192-94

Fetty, William, 192-94

Flower, William, 107-108

Folk, Elizabeth, 190

Forrest, Dean Thomas, 80

Forrest, Henry, 78

Forrester, Robert, 80

Frankesh, John, 127

Frith, John, 62-64

Fust, Thomas, 137-38

G

George, Agnes, 178-79

Gerrand, 74

Ghest, Laurence, 47-48

Glover, Hugh, 43

Glover, John, 139-42

Glover, Robert, 139-42

Glover, William, 139-42

Godly Woman, A, 48-49

Gough, Alexander, 194-95

Gourlay, Norman, 79

Gwin, John, 180

H

Habensa, Bishop of, 26

Hale, William, 138

Halliwell, William, 178-79

Hamilton, Catherine, 79

Hamilton, James, 79

Hamilton, Patrick, 77-78

Harwood, Stephen, 135, 137-38

Hawkes, Thomas, 109-113

Hewet, Andrew, 64-65

Hippolitus, 14

Hook, Richard, 135

Hooper, John, 92-94

Hornes, Joan, 178

Hudson, Thomas, 196-97

Hullier, John, 185-86

Hunter, William, 99-103

Hurst, Edmund, 178-79

Huss, John, 38-40

Hut, Catherine, 178

I

Ignatius, 10-11

Iveson, Thomas, 129, 131-32

J

Jackson, Ralph, 178-79

James, 5, 7-8

Jerome, 74

Jerome of Prague, 40-41

Joannes, 15

John, 9-10

K

Keillor, Friar, 80

Kerby, 75-76

King, George, 135, 138

L

Lambert, John, 69-72

Lashford, Joan, 135, 138

Latimer, Hugh, 147-56

Launder, John, 128-31

Laverock, Hugh, 177-78

Lawrence, 17-18

Leaf, John, 122-24

Lewis, Joyce, 190-92

Leyes, Thomas, 135, 138

Liberatus, 26

Lithgow, William, 28-29

Luther, Martin, 51-55

M
Malchus, 15
Marcus, Bishop of Arethusa, 23
Mark, 5
Marsh, George, 106-107
Martianus, 15
Martin, Isaac, 29-30
Martina, 14
Matthew, 7
Maturus, 12
Maximianus, 15
Metrus, 15
Middleton, Humphry, 127
Milderdale, Richard, 43
Miller, Simon, 186-87
Milne, Walter, 85-87
Mordon, James, 46
Munt, Alice, 188-90
Munt, William, 188-90
N
Newman, John, 133, 135
Nicetas, 24-25
O
Origen, 16
Ormes, Cicely, 187-88
P
Packingham, Patrick, 134
Palmer, Julius, 179-80
Pammachius, 14
Parnam, Lawrence, 178-79
Paul, 9
Pepper, Elizabeth, 178-79
Perpetua, 13-14
Peter, 9
Polycarp, 12
Pontianus, 14
Powel, 74
Purchase, William, 189-90

Pygot, Robert, 143-44
Q
Quinta, 15
Quiritus, 14
R
Ridley, Bishop, 144-60
Roberts, Father, 46
Rogatus, 26
Rogers, John, 89-90
Routh, John, 178-79
Rusticus, 26
S
Sabas, 24
Sanctus of Vienne, 12
Sanders, Lawrence, 90-92
Saturnius, Bishop of Toulouse, 17
Sautre, Sir William, 34-36
Savonarola, Jerome, 44
Searles, George, 178-79
Septimus, 26
Seraion, 15
Servus, 26
Severus, 22
Sheterden, Nicholas, a 127
Silverside, Agnes, 189-90
Simon, 5
Simon the apostle, 5
Simpson, Duncan, 80
Smith, Robert, 135, 137
Spurge, Richard, 176-77
Spurge, Thomas, 176-77
Stephen, Bishop of Rome, 17
Straiton, David, 79
Sturdy, James, 43
T
Tankervil, George, 135-37
Taylor, Rowland, 94-99
Telemachus, 26-27

Tewkesbury, John, 61-62
Thacker, Thomas, 127
Thackvill, Elizabeth, 178
Theodora, 16
Theodorus, 22-23
Thomas, 5
Thorpe, William, 37-38
Tims, 176-77
Trevisam, James, 124
Tylsworth, William, 46
Tyndale, William, 67-69
U
Urice, Bishop of, 26
V
Vesie, William, 129
W
Wade, John, 135, 138
Waid, Christopher, 127-28
Waldenses, the, 58-59
Wallace, Adam, 83-85
Warne, Elizabeth, 135-36
Warne, John, 108-109
Waste, Joan, 181
Watts, Thomas, 115-18
Wendelmuta, 57-58
White, Rawlins, 103-106
White, William, 41-43
Wishart, George, 81-83
Wolsey, William, 143-44
Woodman, Richard, 182-84
Wycliffe, John, 31-34
Wye, Henry, 178-79
Z
Zwingle, Ulric, 55-57